Journeys
of Friendship

Journeys
of Friendship
30
TRUE STORIES
of Kindred Connections

Collected by Allison Gappa Bottke
Founder of the God Allows U-Turns Project,
with Cheryll Hutchings

BARBOUR
PUBLISHING

Compiled by Shannon Hill.

ISBN 1-59310-686-6

The author is represented by Alive Communications, Inc., 7680 Goddard St., Suite 200, Colorado Springs, Colorado 80920.

Published by Barbour Publishing, Inc., P.O. Box 719, Uhrichsville, Ohio 44683
www.barbourbooks.com

Our mission is to publish and distribute inspirational products offering exceptional value and biblical encouragement to the masses.

Member of the
Evangelical Christian
Publishers Association

Printed in the United States of America.
5 4 3 2 1

Contents

Introduction. 7

Crossing the Bridge of Friendship

   by Elizabeth Turner. 9

Angel in a Snowsuit by Ellen Javernick 13

The Hug Fund by Cheryl Norwood 16

Civil War Friends by Margaret Sayler. 20

Friendship Bread by Amy Jenkins 23

Roses and Silver Maples by D. L. Young 26

Mr. J. by Kathryn Howard. 30

Mercy's Time by Julie Saffrin 33

Love Thy Neighbor by Rusty Fischer. 36

The Wal-Mart Missionary

   by Patty Smith Hall 41

Forgiveness at Pearl Harbor

   by Susan Farr Fahncke. 43

My New York Angel by Allison Gappa Bottke 46

A Secret Code by Sara A. DuBose. 52

The Neighbors Next Door by Karen Strand. 54

When the World Became One

   by Norka Blackman-Richards 58

TUSLOG Det 66 by Jacque E. Day 61

Miracle on Mercer Street by Carol Genengels. 65

A Father's Love by Michael T. Powers 69

Faith at Iwo Jima by Nancy Cripe 72

My Buddy Jules by Paul Madison 76

Someone Else's Child by Janice Thompson. 82

Just Keep Up with Me by Carlin Hertz 86

The Cross on the Chalkboard

   by Mary Ellen Gudeman 91

Cyber Witness by Cindy Appel 95

Nicholas by Susan Farr Fahncke 98

The Smiles of Children by Jennifer Bottke. 103

Twinkle, Twinkle, Little Star by Jeanne Zornes 106

Smiley by Karen Garrison 110

Angel of Kindness by Linda Knight. 116

The Ivory Quill by Darlyn Bush 118

About the God Allows U-Turns Project Founder 123

About the Contributors 124

Introduction

Can you remember the first friend you met in elementary school? Maybe she shared her "lucky" pencil with you, then a smile, and later, her secrets. Maybe he had the best tree house in the second grade and insisted you come over every afternoon to help "work" on it—which translated into many fun hours of banging nails into old boards.

The thirty compelling stories in this book, the very best of the God Allows U-Turns collection, offer a glimpse into extraordinary acts of friendship that are found in the minutiae of everyday life. Whether it's the lasting bond of lifelong friends or the new ties of sworn enemies who have found a way to love each other, kindred connections are unveiled in important, God-inspired moments.

These moments make up the milestones along the journey. We mark our days and the passing of time not by accomplishments or possessions, but by the relationships that have impacted our lives. And the friends God has blessed us with fuel our journey. Read on and experience the God-inspired moments in these thirty stories. Perhaps they'll serve as poignant reminders of your own milestone relationships.

Crossing the Bridge of Friendship
by Elizabeth Turner, Oakville, Ontario

Maybe it was his crippled stature that first drew me to the old man across the road. My years as an ICU nurse had developed my high level of interest in anyone with an obvious debilitation. The level of his impairment was extreme. The arthritis, so apparent, had bowed his limbs to a grotesque degree. On the very few occasions that I saw him out of his motorized wheelchair, he was a piteous site. He was shrunken to perhaps four feet, and it is difficult to aptly describe the severity of his body's betrayal. His age was difficult to decipher, but his eldest son, a strapping six-footer, appeared to be approaching his thirties.

Their arrival in our neighborhood caused many tongues to wag. It wasn't so much the fact that they were East Indian by nationality. Our typically Canadian street represented the best of our nation's "tossed salad." It was, perhaps, the number of inhabitants in the home that we thought odd. There seemed to be at least three adult couples residing in the home. Making things even more intriguing was that fact that the three women residents were all in various stages of pregnancy.

As I customarily do with all new arrivals on our street, I delivered a home-baked pie and welcome card shortly after they moved in. With a distinct language barrier, we depended on body language to express ourselves. After my initial introduction, very few words were spoken between my new neighbors and myself. Waves and smiles were the best we could achieve.

Through their first winter, I seldom saw the old man outside, but he maintained a strident vigil at the lovely picture window at the front of the home.

By the spring, three new inhabitants had made an appearance. With interest—or nosiness, depending on your outlook—I watched the arrangement of the household. Leaving early each morning were the three young men and two of the wives. By eight each morning, as I took my own children to school, the old man would be perched in their driveway, one child strapped to his back and another occupying each of his arms. I always waved.

The two little girls and the tiny boy were gorgeous babies. All had sooty lashes that accentuated their beauty. The old man would smile and nod his head as I admired his charges. By 9:30, the remaining wife would come and take one child at a time, presumably for feeding and diapering. Throughout the rest of the day, it appeared the babies were on a rotating schedule. While one was inside, the old man would have one on his back and one in his lap. At the end of the day, the other adults would arrive home, and the old man would be released from his duties. Remarkably, this was the time when, from his wheelchair, he would toil in the garden. In short order, my appreciation of the old man grew.

Over the course of the next few years, I watched from the sidelines. The children grew rapidly, each delighting in the old man's attentions. The highlight of the day appeared to be "The Race." Placing one child on his lap, he would put his chair in high gear and rush to the corner. The remaining two would count off the amount of time that it took and, in a language I didn't understand, urge the old man to go even faster on their turn. It was a sight to behold. Unable to turn away, I occasionally felt like a voyeur, vicariously feeling a bit of their joy.

While leaving the house one day, I was met with a curious spectacle. Standing in their driveway were the three sons, their wives, and the children. They all had an unmistakable air of sadness about them. As I watched, the entire group moved toward me from across the street. Bowing, the eldest of the sons handed me an envelope. My heart was pounding as I saw the tear-swollen faces of the three women. It didn't take long for the realization of their loss to set in. No more would I delight in the antics of the children and their grandfather.

My grief was genuine, and I shook each of the sons' hands in turn, unable to stop my own tears. The "home wife," as I had come to call her, came forward and, for the first time, looked me directly in the eye. Not a word was spoken, but when I felt her arms around my shoulders, our hearts spoke words that neither of us could find. I prayed silently for God to comfort them all in this time of sorrow.

After delivering the kids to school, I realized that I had

driven with the unopened envelope clutched in my hand. Opening it, I was surprised to see the very card that I had presented to them four years earlier. I started crying, thinking of the dear present that the old man had left for me. Boldly scrawled across the front of the card, he had left me the one word that he knew I would understand—FRIEND.

Angel in a Snowsuit
by Ellen Javernick, Loveland, Colorado

Time didn't have much meaning for Mrs. Ramsey. Her only daughter, a darling little girl with long black braids and a sparkling smile, died of leukemia when she was in second grade, and her husband died just a few years later. She felt old, unloved, and unneeded. One day was pretty much the same as the next, and Valentine's Day crept up almost unnoticed.

She was surprised one February morning when she answered the door and saw a rosy-cheeked boy of five or six standing on her doorstep. He was stuffed into a bright blue snowsuit. In his mittened hands he held a bunch of cheery red carnations "and baby's breath, too," marveled Mrs. Ramsey. The little boy pushed the bouquet at Mrs. Ramsey and dashed off down the street before she had time to protest that she had no one to send her flowers. She carried the bouquet inside and looked for a card that might explain the gift. She found a red construction-paper heart in the folds of the paper wrapped around the flowers. "We Love You" was carefully printed on the handmade card. It was signed, "The Children of Edgemont School."

Mrs. Ramsey didn't know quite what to make of the gift. *I haven't,* she admitted to herself, *been especially nice to the Edgemont boys and girls.*

She'd even gotten crabby and scolded the children who walked past her house on their way to school. She'd called the principal to complain about their noisy laughter on the playground and shaken her broom at them when they stomped through puddles on her sidewalk. She'd been furious when she found a small snow angel on the front lawn. Why would they send her a Valentine card?

She promised herself she'd try to be more pleasant. She began chatting with the children when they walked past. She learned their names and admired the work they carried home. In the spring, she started a garden. "So the children would have something pretty to look at," she explained. The following fall she walked over to school and asked the secretary if the school could use a volunteer to help with reading.

Mrs. Ramsey was already a permanent fixture at Edgemont School when I came as a new first-grade teacher. A gaunt but gracious woman, she seemed to spend almost as much time at school as I did. Her smile so warmed the little people she tutored that they begged, "Please, please, can Mrs. Ramsey work with me?" She patted kids' heads and praised their paintings. She called the kindergartners her little angels. She was such a popular volunteer and so effective that I assumed she must be a retired teacher. One day I asked my older teaching partner how long Mrs. Ramsey had been helping at Edgemont.

Allison told me the amazing story of the Valentine card. "Which teacher thought to send her the Valentine flowers?" I asked.

14

Allison laughed. "That's about the strangest part of the story. Miss Perlee was teaching kindergarten then, and she decided it would be nice to send Valentine thank-yous to some of the neighborhood volunteers. She got one of the grocery stores to give her a good price on carnations and then had the children divide them into bouquets. The kids cut out the hearts and copied the words. She gave the flowers to children to drop off on their way home. Little Davey Hamilton was supposed to deliver the flowers to a volunteer on Mrs. Ramsey's street but had trouble with his numbers. Instead of leaving the flowers for the faithful volunteer who lived at 741, he took them to Mrs. Ramsey at 714!"

"Did she ever find out? Mrs. Ramsey, I mean?" I asked Allison.

"Davey admitted his mistake," said Allison, "when he was in sixth grade."

Mrs. Ramsey said it wasn't a mistake. "God knew exactly what He was doing the day He sent me an angel in a snowsuit."

The Hug Fund
by Cheryl Norwood, Canton, Georgia

You would think that getting married somewhat later in life than most couples, Mike and I would have been more established financially. However, neither of us brought much to the marriage cashwise. We had decent jobs but not much in savings. Mike was your typical bachelor before our marriage; that is, he had a new car, expensive furniture, and stereo equipment but no money in the bank. I had been supporting an antique habit and a shoe addiction. But we were comfortable and enjoyed being able to contribute money to several worthy causes on top of our tithe to our local church. God had truly blessed us, and we enjoyed sharing those blessings with others.

Then the bottom fell out. Four months into our marriage, an uninsured driver hit me. Then Mike's company closed its doors. My insurance was limited and did not cover home nursing care for me. Even with the help of our wonderful family and friends, Mike had to stay home with me and missed out on several job opportunities. Finally, we were both able to go back to work, but our meager savings were depleted, and debts had added up.

We knew we would be back on our feet eventually, and we were very grateful for the physical healing God had given me. God had really watched out for us, blessing us not only with my physical healing but with a deepening of our love for each other, as well as with an awareness of all the wonderful people around us.

What could we give back? It was a struggle just to pay our tithe each week. There was no money for anything extra. We stretched those pennies so far that Lincoln screamed! Every time a need came up, we would empty our pockets, but we felt it was so little and the needs were so great. We wanted badly to share God's goodness to us with others.

One day I received a check for just over ten dollars, a rebate on an insurance overpayment. I cashed it and brought the money home. I put it in an antique tea tin on the shelf in the living room. Mike and I decided to start a fund and let God tell us how to spend it. We prayed about this little fund, asking Him to show us how our tiny sum of money could make a difference for Him.

The next week, a friend at work was very depressed. She was recently divorced and feeling overwhelmed by loneliness. She didn't share much with us, but one day as I was going down the hall, I overheard her say, "I feel invisible, like no one would even notice if I just suddenly disappeared." I went home to Mike, and we prayed about it and then decided we would put the ten dollars in a card to her. Since she knew my handwriting, Mike addressed the card. We bought a little encouragement card and wrote a short note and signed it, "God loves you and so do we. You make a difference!"

Not much of a gift, but when I saw my friend at work a few days later, she was just bubbling. She had never shared anything personal with us at work, but around the coffeepot that morning, she told everyone about the card and gift. She said she treated herself and the kids to pizza with the ten dollars (this was ten years ago!), and they had a little party for no reason. She said to us, "I felt like God reached down and gave me a big hug!"

Thus began God's Hug Fund. We would put in leftover change and money saved by using coupons. Occasionally one of us would have a little overtime in our check, and we would pitch that in the tin. Sometimes it would be Mike who would notice someone who needed "a hug from God." Sometimes God showed me a person in need of a hug. We kept it anonymous. We didn't always send a card, and we didn't always give cash; sometimes we bought something and left it. Sometimes it was groceries for a family having hard times. Sometimes it was something silly to get a laugh from a grouch!

Through it all, we learned that you don't need to have a lot to give a lot. We also learned the sweet blessing of giving in secret. When you give in secret, God gets the credit He deserves. Without your pride and the recipient's pride getting in the way, God has room to work!

While we are very grateful to be able to contribute financially to God's work in a bigger way now, we still look for little ways to give out those hugs. The neatest blessing to come out of all this is that we are also more aware of all the little hugs God sends our way. Last week alone I received a smile from a child, a thank-you note, a great afternoon shopping with a friend, a free lunch dropped off by someone who knew I was working through lunch at my desk, and help from a neighbor carrying in the groceries.

Someone's tea tin must be empty, because I think God emptied it out just for me!

Civil War Friends
by Margaret Sayler, Sacramento, California

The Doan family crossed the Missouri creek with aching feet and exhausted bodies. Their journey from Illinois with three wagons had been long. As they approached the large farmhouse, they hoped the owners would put them up for the night.

"Put your horses and wagons in our barn, then join us for dinner," the farmer said, warmly welcoming them.

Inside the house, ten-year-old Julius Doan smelled the roast pork and saw extended tables heaped with food for the farmer and his family, hired help, and the Doans. After the blessing, everyone ate generous portions of meat, mashed potatoes, corn, biscuits, and apple pan dowdy.

The farmer looked around at the six sons and two daughters of Joseph and Anna Doan.

"My family is smaller than yours," he said. "But I have another son. During the war he was a captain for the Confederates. We expect him momentarily."

Julius choked. He looked at John and Jessie, his two older brothers who had just returned from the Civil War. John had even served under Union commander General William T. Sherman. But now these Union men responded to the farmer's announcement with casual smiles, as if they considered Confederates friendly neighbors.

After dinner the family and guests settled in the front parlor where the farmer's daughters played the piano and sang. Normally Julius would have sneaked behind the piano and pulled the young soprano's pigtails, but tonight his stomach churned. When the farmer's son appeared, would there be a fight? Julius hated a showdown. He couldn't understand how the rest of the family kept their composure.

At last the front door opened. Surprisingly, John jumped to his feet. "Matthew!" John cried, his face beaming as the farmer's son entered the room.

"John!" the farmer's son, Matthew, exclaimed. He turned to his father and explained, "John rustled for Sherman's army on the march to Savannah! I was his prisoner."

Mouths flew open. For a moment everyone stared at the two men.

"You treated me well," the farmer's son told John. "We became good friends," he told his father.

Matthew and John shook hands. Julius heard the host family say, "John surely must have treated Matthew well!"

Julius settled back in his chair. He thought about the love his brothers had always shown him. Now he knew what made them so special. He often heard them pray, "God, let your Calvary love pour out through our lives." God had answered their prayers.

Remembering this story in later years stirred the heart of my grandfather, Julius. God's great love brought Jesus from the splendor of heaven to pay a devastating price for the world's sin. Anticipating the time when he would see Jesus, Julius knew he would marvel at what Jesus did. This gave him confidence to believe God readily answers our prayers.

As Matthew sat down, surrounded by his family and the Doans, an impish smile lit young Julius's face. He decided if that girl sang again, he'd find a way to steal over and pull her hair.

Friendship Bread
by Amy Jenkins, Wauwatosa, Wisconsin

My mom dropped off a plastic bag with taupe-colored goop in it and a recipe for "Friendship Bread." It takes ten days to make this cake-like bread, which is reported to have Amish origins.

Every twelve hours I was to shake the bag and on some days, add something to it. It was imperative, or so said the instructions, that this be done on schedule. By day four, I was muttering about how stupid this was. "No, I can't sleep late; I have to get up early to shake my friendship bag." At 7:00 p.m.: "No, we can't stop for ice cream."

When we went to the movies, I took my tote bag containing the required ingredients. While Harrison Ford fought a battle on *Air Force One*, I met my responsibility. At the appropriate time, I poured in a cup of sugar and shook the mixture. As I peeked over my shoulder to be sure that the usher wouldn't catch me, I wondered what they would do if they did catch me. I imagined being banned from Capital Theater. Perhaps they'd post a drawing of a mixing bowl and spoon within a red circle with a line through it. Harrison and I accomplished our missions successfully.

On the last day, I poured my creation into a mixing bowl with the other ingredients to make four loaves. That's where I made my critical mistake. I missed the part where I was first supposed to divide the liquid into five bags and just use one bag at a time. Since I had already poured the whole bag of liquid in, I was committed to baking all twenty loaves of bread. *What in heaven's name will I do with twenty loaves of bread?* I lamented silently.

In the middle of baking the last batch, I heard the radio announcer report that Habitat for Humanity was starting their housing blitz the next day and was asking for volunteers. I was pleased to learn I could volunteer to sponsor a snack.

The bread was moist, sweet, and topped with a crunchy cinnamon mixture. I sliced up nineteen loaves, spread them attractively on trays, wrapped them in plastic wrap, and took them to the Habitat work site.

Every year since, they have asked me to sponsor a snack. In recent years, I have brought muffins, fruit, and cupcakes. They still ask me to bring that delicious friendship bread, but I don't have a bag of squishy goop. I have no idea how it starts—someone would have to give me a batch exactly eleven days before the start of the blitz. What's the chance of that happening—again?

Last July my new neighbor came over as I was baking muffins. She asked me what I was doing. When I explained about the building blitz, she asked me how I got involved in Habitat for Humanity. After the story of my accidental volunteer work, she told me, "The only way that story could be true is if God had planned it. And God must have planted me here as your new neighbor as well," she said, shaking her head in further amazement as she went on to tell me that she and her mother's friends pass around the friendship batter every year, and that I should look for a baggie of fermenting goop about the beginning of next July, just in time for the next Habitat building blitz.

Roses and Silver Maples
by D. L. Young, Cleveland, Tennessee

We all lived on the same street in the same neighborhood. Each house was identical. Each had a five-foot silver maple planted in the small patch of lawn between the sidewalk and the street. The country flourished, progressing at an astounding rate. It was the sixties.

I lived in the eighth house on the right from the city end of the street with my mother, Joann, my father, Woody, and my big brother, Lee. Our twelve-hundred-square-foot ranch-style home never had a thing out of place. In our house, you could literally eat off the kitchen floor without worrying about eating dirt. My mom was the best housekeeper in town.

Each day, my dad came home around 6:00 from his job at the car dealership and kissed my mother hello. He was in charge of eight "bump and paint" men. I was proud because, in my seven-year-old eyes, my dad was *the boss*.

"How was your day, squirt?" he'd ask me, swinging me high in the air.

"Great, Daddy," I'd reply. "Guess what happened today?"

It never made a difference what happened; he always listened. We sat on the front stoop, and he wouldn't say a thing until I'd finished my rambling. Occasionally I would have to pause for him to wave to a neighbor or to a kid passing by on a bike who'd yell, "Hiya, Woody."

Two doors down from us on the left lived Greg and Cathy and their four kids, all under eight years old. As a kid myself, I wondered about them because I seldom saw any of the children. If they were in the front yard playing and I waved, they immediately ran into the backyard, out of sight.

"Cathy sure has her hands full with those four kids," I heard my dad tell my mom.

"Somebody needs to do something about that husband of hers," my mom replied. I wondered what kind of something she meant. Late one autumn afternoon I found out.

I was skating up and down the driveway in the new skates I had received for a good report card. The sound of Greg's rattly old Chevy pickup caught my attention. He pulled into their driveway and left the engine running. Soon he reappeared from the house, arms loaded with boxes. Cathy ran after him.

"Greg, please don't leave. I'll do better."

"You're worthless, woman," he yelled. "You can't do one thing right, and you're the worst mother in the world." Cathy was crying. She tugged at Greg's shirt as he passed her.

"Please?" She held on. I stood silent under the silver maple, not believing what I saw. Then he slugged her, and she fell to the ground.

I fumbled across the narrow sidewalk into the safety of the

grass and ran to get my dad.

"Daddy, Daddy, come quick! Greg just hit Cathy. They're fighting!"

By the time my dad got to the front door, Greg was gone, clunking down the street in his beat-up Chevy, never to be seen again.

"Stay here, squirt."

Cathy hugged her silver maple, tears flowing. My dad pried her away from the tree, and Cathy wrapped her arms around his neck and sobbed.

"It will be okay." He patted her back, holding her until she pulled away from him.

My parents' faces were solemn at the dinner table that night. My brother and I ate our food in silence. We knew they were contemplating solutions. We could tell, because my mother's hand rested on top of my father's arm, and a warm, loving look waited for his answer.

Daddy stabbed his fork into the air. "I've been meaning to hire a secretary. The paperwork is getting to be too much for me to handle." My mother smiled.

"Rita Dumont, on the next street over, said she wanted to find a job close to home," Mom added. "Maybe I'll talk to her about baby-sitting. We can pay her for a couple of months. Cathy will never have to know. Right?" Mother lifted her eyebrows to Lee and me. "Right?" she said again.

"Um, right." We smiled at her.

28

The next day I skated again. Practice makes perfect, and I was determined to master the art of staying erect. A white panel van pulled into Cathy's driveway, and a man got out carrying a big, long package. After he left, Cathy walked toward our house.

"Smell," she said to me, opening the box. Inside were a dozen white roses, perfectly bloomed and swimmingly fragrant. I had never seen (or smelled) anything so beautiful. Cathy must have felt the same, for a wide smile spread across her face. I wondered if the corners of her mouth would reach her ears. Then she showed me the card. It said, "Keep your chin up! Woody and Joann."

My heart burst with love and pride for my dad and mom.

Today I am forty-seven years old. My parents are in their eighties, living in that same brick ranch. The silver maples have grown to wondrous heights, and my dad still makes every effort to help whomever he can.

The image of Cathy receiving those roses lives in my mind like it was yesterday. And the scent of roses makes me smile with a delicious secret I will always hold dear to my heart.

Mr. J.

by Kathryn Howard, Rochester, New York

"Don't worry about Mr. J. Just tell him what you're doing; then go on to someone else," the Manhattan nursing home administrator told me, pointing to a gentleman in the corner alone.

"Why can't I give him a letter?" I asked.

"Well, he's blind, so why waste it?" she said.

"But these pictures are made of construction paper pasted onto more construction paper. They have texture. Can't I give him one and tell him what he's feeling with his fingers?" I was determined not to exclude anyone.

The administrator sighed. "Go ahead, but he won't talk to you. He hasn't talked to anyone since September eleventh."

I walked to Mr. J. and sat down beside him. "Mr. J., I'm Kathryn. I want to give you a picture that was made by a preschooler near Rochester. The kids there have been visiting people like you. They feel like the residents are extra grandmas and grandpas," I explained. "When they found out about what happened on September eleventh, they were worried about grandmas and grand-pas here in the city and wanted to do something. They want you to know they're thinking about you and you're in their prayers."

Mr. J. was silent. I took his hand and moved it to the paper in front of him.

"This is a picture of a flower in a flowerpot." I moved his fingers over the flower petals. "The flower is bright purple." His fingers went to the stem. "The stem is green." He moved down to the flowerpot. "The flowerpot is orange. And there is a bright blue sky and a golden-yellow sun shining down on the flower." Mr. J.'s hand stopped moving.

"This picture was made by Davy, and he's four. He wrote a message on the back of the picture. It says, 'I am hoping for you.' "

Mr. J.'s face crumpled. His sightless eyes filled with tears. He hoarsely whispered, "I felt it."

I didn't quite understand. "I'm sorry, Mr. J.; you felt what?"

"When they fell. I felt them fall," he explained softly.

"Oh, Mr. J., I am so sorry." My tears mixed with his as we cried for the lost souls and hopes and dreams that died on that awful day. Then we talked about being scared and not knowing what to do. He told me about sitting in the TV room, hearing about the plane crashes and finally the fall of the World Trade Center towers.

"I knew before they said it on the TV," Mr. J. remarked. "I felt the vibrations through the floor. I didn't know what it was. I never felt anything like it before. I was so scared. How could someone do that to us? Why?"

I had no answer. We sat for a while longer holding hands.

Then it was time to go. I hugged him. "Please take care of yourself, Mr. J."

He smiled and patted my hand. "I'll be fine now, girl, don't you worry. And you give that Davy a big thank-you for me. Wait a minute. I'll do it myself. I'll braille that boy a note and tell him myself. Can I do that? Can you get a letter back to him?"

I laughed. "You bet I can. And won't you make him happy! You write that note, and I'll come back and get it from you."

Mr. J. was silent, and I got up. He leaned forward suddenly and spoke again.

"Maybe this is the good that can come out of the evil. Maybe just having folks reach out to one another is the message we're supposed to get. They can bend us, but they will never break us. I'll tell Davy that in my note."

"You do that, Mr. J. And I'll make sure that everyone else gets the message, too."

I gathered up my things to leave. The administrator took me aside.

"What on earth did you do to Mr. J.?" she quizzed. "This is the first time he's said anything more than yes or no since September eleventh. What did you say to him?"

I shrugged my shoulders. "It wasn't me; it was the message Davy sent that helped him to speak. I was just here to make sure Mr. J. got the letter."

"Then God bless Davy," she said as she smiled at me.

I smiled back. "Amen."

Mercy's Time
by Julie Saffrin, Excelsior, Minnesota

She was nearly my mother-in-law. That she is not had nothing to do with her. The two years we knew each other, Doris was easy to know. I was nineteen; she was in her late fifties.

She welcomed my presence into her son's life and treated me like a daughter in hers. Our mutual love for her son was our commonality and made our bond strong.

Invited to their world, I shared meals and trips to the cabin. A year later a depleted box of tissue accompanied Doris and me on the way home after we left her son at boot camp.

To fend off long winter nights, I visited Doris after work. We had warm talks of possibilities. She, a patient right-hander, taught me, a left-hander with dreams of marriage, to crochet a bedspread. I even helped her pick out a puppy at the Humane Society; Doris named her Precious.

When the engagement was announced, her gifts of a silverware chest and milk-glass butter dish started the hope chest. Though she often said she was a terrible cook, my first recipe of Mexican stew, which I still make, came from her.

When the engagement was broken, so, too, was my friendship

with Doris. Awkward and young, I didn't know how to say good-bye. So I didn't.

On occasion, in the twenty years since, she would come to mind. As hard as I tried, I could not put her out of my head. I knew I would never forgive myself if something happened to her before I said I was sorry for my rude behavior.

On a Florida vacation, while I read a novel filled with estrangements and reconciliations, she visited my thoughts again. Whether Doris chose to forgive me or not, the inevitable was here. It was time to apologize for the abrupt severing of our friendship.

I knew that Doris's sister, Elsie, lived in town, although I had no idea where. A long walk with my index finger through the phone directory found her. It took me two weeks to muster the courage to call.

Elsie informed me that the years had been harsh to Doris. She had gone through a divorce, several seizures, brain surgery, and now was in the final stage of emphysema. When I asked if it would be all right to write her, her sister said that it would be fine.

Now that I had permission, I was terrified. I had broken her son's heart and burst a seemingly perfect dream of togetherness. *Surely she must hate me. Certainly no good will come from a simple handwritten apology,* I thought.

A sleepless week went by. It was no use. Until I put pen to paper, there would be no peace in my heart.

Lord, give me the words to convey my sorriness was my quiet plea.

"Dear Doris, I know it's been many years since you and I last had contact," I began. It took until page 3 to get to my reason for writing. "I know when I broke his heart, I broke part of yours. Knowing you like I once did, you probably forgave me years ago, but what good is an apology that no one hears? I'm sorry for the pain and the way I ended it all," I wrote. I asked for forgiveness; if she found it in her heart to do so, I wanted to hear it.

A week went by, two, before her familiar curly handwriting appeared in my mailbox. The envelope was heavy. My fears resurfaced. I prepared for a severe lecture.

"You can't know what your letter has done for me," she wrote. "Came at the right time, too." Her letter was delightful. She gladly accepted my apology, forgave me, recalled some happy times, and even asked for a recipe. Her words lightened a burden I had carried too long.

As I put the letter back in the envelope, a picture of Precious slipped out. On the back she had written, "Remember when you went with me to pick her out? She died last year. I miss her so." I thought of that dog. Like the Mexican stew, it made me happy that a part of our togetherness had carried into Doris's life, too.

God's merciful timing played a part in Doris and me settling things. Two months later her sister called to tell me the sad news that Doris had passed away. I'm grateful God knew I needed to say good-bye.

Love Thy Neighbor
by Rusty Fischer, Orlando, Florida

When I finally got home from work that night, I wasn't too surprised to see the door unlocked. My wife had stayed home from work complaining of an upset stomach. I had called home during the day and gotten the answering machine each time. I hadn't been too concerned, because she had mentioned a trip to the walk-in clinic to see if they could give her something to help.

All that changed when I saw the broom lying in the middle of the floor. My wife was a confirmed neat freak. It was totally unlike her to leave a broom lying in the middle of the floor. Calling out her name, I noticed other things out of kilter as well. The coffee machine was still on, with strong-smelling black coffee still inside. I switched it off with a shaking hand. Her purse was on the kitchen table, her keys nearby.

I called her name loudly, insistently, as I ran through our two-bedroom apartment, stopping at our bathroom. Plastic wrappers littered the floor with strange symbols and fancy medical terminology covering them. Measurements. Liters. Saline. It looked like something out of an ER episode.

Just then a knock sounded at the door. I opened it without

hesitation and was shocked to see that it was our upstairs neighbor. "What do you want?" I asked flippantly of the scraggly college girl who caused us so much grief. Her revolving boyfriends and their big clomping feet and her loud music and late-night parties were the source of many sleepless nights for my wife and me.

Although my wife was always quick to point out that "we were young once, too," and how hard it was for a single girl to live alone these days, I knew that some girls were just plain born bad. My wife would frown. "God doesn't allow His children to be born bad," she'd say sternly. "He doesn't do that. Something made her that way. It's up to us to understand her, help her, and be patient with her. Every one of God's children has a purpose; so does she."

All I ever saw, though, was a noisy brat who kept us up late at night. She was the first person I'd thought of when I saw the broom in the middle of the floor that afternoon. It was the same broom I used to knock on the ceiling at 2:00 a.m. to get her to quiet down!

"Don't you want to know where your wife is?" she asked incredulously. The plot of a true-crime murder mystery shot through my mind. Had all of my complaints to the apartment complex management finally gotten to this scrawny girl who favored rap CDs with thumping bass? Had she taken my griping personally and hired one of her many questionable boyfriends to kidnap my wife and thus silence the constant complaints? Had my good-hearted and patient wife simply gone up with yet another peace offering in the form of a cake, not to mention a little friendly "witnessing," one too many times and happened upon a drug bust gone bad?

I almost said, "What have you done with her?" Instead, I simply waited for an explanation.

"I'll explain while you drive to the hospital," she said instead. They were the last words I ever expected to hear from her mouth.

"I woke up late," she said shyly as I drove through town, gritting my teeth at slow drivers and grunting audibly at stop-lights that always seemed to see me coming. "I did some laundry, straightened up, and then turned on the stereo real loud."

"Big surprise," I scoffed, hunched over the wheel.

"Well," she said in defense, "I knew you two yuppies would be at your nine-to-five jobs, so I was very surprised to hear thumping underneath me. I looked out the window, and sure enough, your wife's car was still in the parking lot."

"How did you know my wife's car?" I asked, still slightly suspicious.

"I ran into her one day not long after you'd first moved in," she explained, pointing out the way to the hospital. "She asked directions to the mailbox and loaned me five dollars," she added sheepishly as I sighed aloud. "Anyway, I figured she was taking the day off, so I turned down the music. The thumping kept right on going, quiet and all, but I could tell that's what it was. Finally, I turned the music off altogether, but the thumping just kept right on going. I have to tell you, I got a little peeved. So I stomped downstairs to knock on the door. You know, just to ask your wife what her problem was. I knocked and knocked, but no one answered.

"That freaked me out a little," she admitted. "I knew she'd been knocking on the ceiling. . .and now she wasn't answering? I knew she wasn't afraid of me, having been up to my place so many times with a pound cake or plate of cookies. So I walked over to the rental office and asked them to check on her.

"I followed the manager lady in, and thank God we did. She was passed out on the bathroom floor. There was blood everywhere. I just—"

"Blood?" I shouted, screeching into the huge hospital parking lot. "She had a stomachache this morning and—"

"She'd been throwing up all morning," explained the girl. "Something she ate, I guess. Then, when there was nothing left to throw up, she just kept retching. She ruptured a blood vessel in her throat or something and started bleeding. It looked a lot worse than it was, but they wanted to take her to the hospital to get her rehydrated and take some electrolyte tests."

The emergency room was crowded, and we sat in silence until a young doctor escorted us back to see my wife. Seeing her in a hospital bed surrounded by IV tubes and beeping machines as they monitored her rehydration and blood pressure tore into my heart just as fear clawed at my stomach.

What if this skinny, noisy rap fan upstairs hadn't been home? What if she'd simply ignored my wife's thumping and gone out shopping at the mall for the afternoon? What if my wife hadn't loaned her that five dollars so that this young girl would remember her car?

What if I'd been as believing and trusting as my wife?

My wife's eyes flickered in recognition, and a warm smile crossed her pale face. The instinct to run to her and shelter her in my arms was so strong that I nearly leaped across the room. I had not been her protector that day, though. I had been off in my little office with my little job, too caught up in my own troubles to think twice about her "tummy ache"—a problem that no doubt was caused by the questionable all-you-can-eat seafood buffet from the night before.

No, it was our young neighbor who'd been her hero on this day. Despite my protective, loving urges, I stepped aside while at the same time gently prodding the young girl forward. She looked at me hesitantly, and when I nodded, she sprang forward to hug the older "yuppie" woman with whom she'd so quickly bonded.

As I watched the two women hug, I realized that I was finally witnessing the very embodiment of faith. And I thanked God for a wife who lived first to do His will—loving her neighbor as herself. . .in spite of my actions. Where I had always seen a scruffy, scrappy, noisy teenager, my wife had always seen one of God's children. A human being. A person. Perhaps even a friend. Now I was seeing the results of a friendship, a friendship that in all probability had saved my wife's life, and it brought tears to my eyes.

The Wal-Mart Missionary
by Patty Smith Hall, Hiram, Georgia

"Young lady, would you like a little Bible?" Bill has become somewhat of a fixture at our local Wal-Mart. For as long as anyone can remember, he has sat on the wooden bench right inside the entrance, handing out paper Bibles for anyone willing to take one.

"Son, this here tells you all about the Lord."

Time has caught up with Bill over the past few years. Two heart attacks and a stroke can do that to the human body. Curly black hair now has more salt than pepper in it. His gait, though purposeful, has slowed. Pain shadows his expression when he thinks no one is watching. But his eyes, those mirrors to the soul, still glow like fire-flies in a mason jar.

"Here you go, sir."

Over a month's time, Bill hands out thousands of tracts to folks who slow down enough to accept his kind offer. Others pleasantly refuse, but most simply smirk as they hurry out the door. Bill just shakes his head and turns to the next person. And on the fifteenth of every month, he calls a local bookstore and orders more booklets.

"Ma'am, can I give your little girl a Bible?"

I'm not sure why, but Bill has been on my heart lately. It could be that I've noticed the empty bench a lot more lately. Maybe I've missed the little song and dance we always do when he tries to give me a booklet. It never fails; he holds out the Book with the sweetest smile on his face.

Grinning back, I remind him that I'm a believer, and I tell him to give it to someone who doesn't know the Lord. And like clockwork, that's how things started today. But the Lord is patient with people like me, and as usual, I felt the urge to talk for a while. I started with the question that had been burning in the back of my mind since the first time I saw Bill: "Why?"

I mean, let's face it. Wal-Mart isn't exactly the first place that pops into my head when I think "mission field." My mind goes to Africa or Russia. Someplace far off where the Word of God is oppressed. Even the local battered women's shelter seemed a more appropriate place for spreading the gospel than a discount store. But not to Bill.

The wrinkles around his eyes grew deeper as he glanced over at the crowds gathered around the automatic doors. "Patty, these folks live and die right here in Hiram. Some of them will never see the inside of a church. But they're here buying groceries or something else. So we need to bring God to them." Bill turned to me, the familiar Book resting in his hand.

Once again, I had put my Lord in a neat little box. Staring at the Book in Bill's outstretched palm, I took it, a gentle reminder from my heavenly Father that His mission field is not a geographical place—but a human heart.

Forgiveness at Pearl Harbor
by Susan Farr Fahncke, Kaysville, Utah

Last March my husband and I spent our anniversary in Hawaii. One of the sights I was most eager to see was the Pearl Harbor memorial. As we waited for our group's turn for the tour, Marty and I heard that a survivor of the bombing would speak in the courtyard. We hurried over to listen.

Dr. Joe Morgan, still handsome at seventy-nine, spoke softly but intensely as he described the nightmare attack of the Japanese on Pearl Harbor. Joe had been stationed on the southwestern shore of Ford Island, right in the center of Pearl Harbor. That Sunday morning he'd pulled duty in Aircraft Utility Squadron Two. At 7:55 a.m., he heard the planes diving. At first Joe assumed they were the usual planes that came before the aircraft carriers.

Then the bombing began.

The nineteen-year-old Texan was confused by the .25-caliber machine gun bullets that rained down around him. He watched fellow sailors fall, hit and bleeding. His confusion turned to horror and fear. He heard an explosion on the runway and looked up. He saw the symbol of the rising sun on the plane and realized the Japanese Imperial Navy was attacking them.

43

Joe's first instinct was to hide. But seeing other young men scramble for weapons, he felt ashamed of himself. Running outside to face his attackers, Joe saw an abandoned machine gun and took up his post, shaking in his size-eight shoes.

Filled with a deep fury, Joe fired and shot down Japanese planes. Although Joe was a Christian, he was unable to shake off the hatred he felt for the nation that was so shockingly killing many young American men. The battle finally ended, with 2,403 Americans killed. The men didn't know if the Japanese would return, so Joe and others stayed at their posts all night. During the night, Joe said a prayer that changed his life. He promised God that if he survived that war, he would become a preacher.

The attack on Pearl Harbor changed Joe's life. Although he kept his word to God, he never quite overcame his feelings for the Japanese nation. Joe eventually became pastor of the Wailuku Baptist Church in Maui. Two years later, Mitsuo Fuchida came to the island. He had been the commander of the naval air forces that led the attack on Pearl Harbor, beginning with Ford Island, on December 7, 1941. Fifteen years had passed since that attack, but Joe still had mixed feelings. After much turmoil, Joe decided to go and listen to Commander Fuchida. He heard Fuchida tell of becoming a Christian. After Fuchida's talk, Dr. Joe Morgan introduced himself.

Mitsuo Fuchida bowed and said one word, "*Gomenasai*." He said simply, "I am sorry."

What happened next was as important an American

moment as any other in history. Fuchida reached out to shake Joe's hand. As Joe clasped his former enemy's hand, he realized that all the anger and animosity toward this man and his country were gone. God had replaced them with forgiveness. Joe Morgan and Mitsuo Fuchida shook hands as brothers in Christ.

Tears filled our eyes as Marty and I listened to this incredible U-turn story of forgiveness. Once the two men were shooting at each other. Now, brothers in Christ, they would fight common foes: hatred and unforgiving hearts—a U-turn that, God willing, will continue for generations to come.

My New York Angel
by Allison Gappa Bottke, Faribault, Minnesota

Even though I was only fourteen, I was an "old" fourteen. A strong-willed child raised by a single, working mother, I was forced to grow up fast. Plus, full-figured and five feet seven, I always passed for someone years older. And so, when my mother threatened to send me away if I continued to see my eighteen-year-old boyfriend, Jerry,* I took matters into my own hands—and ran away from home.

"There's no way she's going to keep us apart," Jerry said as he handed me the money to buy my airplane ticket and two hundred dollars to tide me over until I found a job. "I made a reservation for you to leave tomorrow. Pack a bag and get out before she gets home. Here's the phone number of my friends in New York. They'll put you up for a while. Call them as soon as you land."

This will show her how serious we are. This was my first plane ride and my first love. The thought of being forbidden to see him was unbearable. The thought of being a fourteen-year-old girl alone in New York City didn't bother me.

Landing at LaGuardia Airport at eight o'clock on a Saturday night was the beginning of a journey that would change my life. Walking excitedly to the pay phone to call Jerry's friends, I thought about this luxurious, newfound freedom. I would find a job, and in a few weeks, Jerry would join me. We'd marry and live happily ever after. As the phone rang, I dreamed of married life, of the idyllic way everything would turn out.

"The number you have reached is not a working number. . . ." I jumped at the sound of the recording. *I must have dialed wrong,* I thought. Trying again, this time more carefully, I began to feel apprehension creep through my body.

"The number you have reached. . ." It was true. The number was disconnected. I hung up the phone and stood very still.

There was no way I could reach Jerry that night, as he had rented a room without a phone. "Okay," I said to myself, "this isn't the end of the world. Find a hotel or a YWCA until you can reach Jerry at work in the morning."

I forced myself to look on the bright side. I was in New York! The Big Apple! And, since it was 1970, my first thought was of Greenwich Village—the city of peace, love, and flower power! I'd find somewhere in the Village where I could stay the night. It mattered little to me that it was getting late and that I reeked of "vulnerable underage runaway."

When I arrived, the Village was aglow in lights, a street festival was under way, and artists lined the corridor. Singers, street dancers, and vendors were everywhere, just like on television. After the taxi, phone calls, subway, and the snack I had at the airport, I still had about one hundred fifty dollars, a lot of money—or so I thought. I stopped at a hotel and was told it was fifty dollars for the night. "How could they?" I gasped. Were hotels really that expensive? Fear began to grip my heart, but I fought it with all my might.

By 11:00 p.m., the street vendors were beginning to close up shop. Artists were packing up, and the warm hum of people hustling and bustling was replaced by another kind of atmosphere. Women in very short dresses appeared. Men with lots of jewelry and fancy cars lined the streets. People passed bottles and strange-smelling cigarettes among themselves. I held tightly to my suitcase and continued to walk, repeating to myself that everything would be fine.

Then I saw her work. Canvas touched by God. Paintings and pencil sketch drawings hung on the fence, the content of which called to me. While I was growing up, Mom often took my siblings and me to the art museum. My heart raced.

"Can I help you?" I looked up to the round, pleasant face of an older woman.

"Did you draw these?" I asked in awe. "I love them! Oh, how I'd love to have talent like that!"

"Everyone has some special talent, my dear. One day you'll find yours," she said. "My name is Tanya. What's yours?"

I can't recall what we talked about next, but eventually I asked if she knew where I might find a YWCA. At that question, she looked me straight in the eye and without hesitation said, "Please, come home for the evening with my daughter, Claudette, and me. We have plenty of room. This city is a difficult place to get around in during the daytime and even worse at night. You can get a room tomorrow."

Concerned by the lack of easy alternatives, I accepted her offer. Today I shudder to think what may have happened to me had I not. There is no doubt in my mind, had I remained on the dangerous streets of New York City, that I would have become another runaway statistic. "Then no harm will befall you, no disaster will come near your tent. For he will command his angels concerning you to guard you in all your ways" (Psalm 91:10–11). The Lord sent my angel. Her name was Tanya Cervone.

The next day I called the warehouse where Jerry worked, only to find out he had been recently fired. Calling my best friend in Cleveland, I learned that the police were looking for me. My fairy tale turned into a nightmare. My world was falling apart, but I was determined to hang on. Determined no one would know how frightened I was.

I found a YWCA in the phone book and planned to check in and immediately hit the streets to find a job. Having watched the Macy's New Year's parade every year, I thought I'd start there. I'd go to Macy's and get a job as a salesclerk. I thanked Tanya for her hospitality and asked for directions. Unbeknownst to me, Tanya had listened in on my frantic phone calls.

"Please stay until you find a job," she said. "I'm sure you'll find something in no time, and then you can get a little apartment. Those rooms at the 'Y' are so small and dingy."

I had to admit the comfort of Tanya's apartment would

definitely be better, not to mention safer, and it would allow me to save some money, so I accepted. I put on the only dress I had brought and asked for directions to Macy's. On my way, I felt certain everything would be okay, even though a sick feeling developed in the pit of my stomach.

Years later I found out that while I was gone that first day, Tanya went through my things, located my mom's name and phone number, and contacted her in Ohio. Tanya assured Mom that I was okay and that the police might get me home but wouldn't be able to keep me there. "She has to go home on her own; otherwise, you'll only lose her again," Tanya told my mom. "Trust me; I think maybe I can reach her."

During the next few days, I was repeatedly turned down for jobs because I didn't have acceptable identification. I grew more and more confused and frightened. Finally, reaching Jerry, I was hardly comforted when he called me a crybaby and said that if I really loved him I'd "get it together and get enough money" to help him come out to join me since he had given me all of his available cash. "Do whatever you have to do," he hissed at me over the phone. "You're in New York City. Figure something out soon. I've gotta get out of here, and you owe me," he said, hanging up on me.

Unable to stand the fear any longer, I tearfully confided in Tanya. Never before had I shared such intimate feelings with an adult and been so totally accepted. She spoke of what it was like as an artist, what it was like to create these paintings from her mind's eye. She talked of her life in another country and her own challenges, and she encouraged me to talk about mine. She asked me serious questions, personal questions, and she really listened to my responses. It was as though a dam had burst. We talked for hours. I never knew that kind of communication existed. I went home a few days later of my own free will.

I could have been a thief—or worse—yet she took me in. She gave me the heavenly protection of her heart and home, unconditionally. I never saw Tanya again, yet our Christmas cards and letters were as consistent as the seasons until she passed away a few years ago.

When I learned of her death, I cried first, then smiled at her memory. She reached out and protected a vulnerable, frightened teenager. She exhibited the love of Christ in the truest and purest form.

*Name changed

A Secret Code
by Sara A. DuBose, Montgomery, Alabama

"A code?" Bob asked.

"Sure, why not?" Sonny answered. "You ask the questions, and I'll knock out the answers on the telephone receiver. Look, if it's yes, I'll knock three times; and if it's no, I'll knock once, like this."

Sonny Paterson rapped the receiver.

"Roger. I read you loud and clear," Bob said. "I'll call you Tuesday afternoon around five o'clock. Now, before we hang up, let's pray."

The prayer was short, but as Bob prayed, Sonny tried to commit the next few days to God. The flight from Montgomery to Houston would take no longer than the surgery—about three hours. But coming out of the operating room, Sonny would be minus a voice box, his communication cut to a knock, a nod, or a piece of paper and pencil. Later Sonny might want special laryngeal speech lessons, but for now his one objective was to have the Texas surgeon cut his cancer away.

"Amen," Bob said.

"Amen," Sonny replied. "I'll be waiting to hear from you on Tuesday."

Sonny Paterson—a prominent businessman and active layman in the church—had only three more days to talk. How could he speak everything on his mind? How could he tell his wife and family how much they meant to him? There would still be communication, but what if he couldn't learn the tricky speech method the physician described?

Sonny tried to shut off the pessimism. He'd had troubles before, and God had never let him down. At the same time, Sonny knew that a person's heart can accept something while his mind and body still want to rebel.

Tuesday came. The papers were in order. Blood pressure, temperature, pulse—all checked and found normal. Waiting, saying good-bye, rolling to the operating room on a stretcher. Then nothing until waking up with a dry, hollow feeling of having something missing. Smiles, hand-holding. It was over, the offending cancer removed.

The ring came later. Sonny checked his watch and reached for the phone. It was five o'clock.

"Sonny? Bob Strong. Is it all over?"

Knock, knock, knock, came the reply.

"Are you in much pain?"

Knock.

"Sonny, I have one more question. Has God stood with you? Have you felt His grace and presence through all this?"

There was a pause, and then it started. Not once, not three times, but again and again and again and again came the knocking until Bob Strong closed the conversation with another loud "Amen."

The Neighbors Next Door
by Karen Strand, Lacey, Washington

It's Saturday morning. Sunlight falls into my bedroom, drawing my eyes to the soft pastels of my wallpaper, then to the window where I can see the peak of the rooftop next door. The Coles' rooftop. My thoughts turn to the latest neighborhood news: Kristy has had her baby.

Kristy. Fifteen years old and an unwed mother. Although the Coles have lived next door for several months, I don't know them. But I have heard that Kristy's stepdad, Ron, has an eight-year-old son, Chad, from a previous marriage. And that Kristy's mom, Sue, has a teenage son, Todd, from her first marriage. Next there's two-year-old Scott, who was born to Ron and Sue. Now Kristy has made Sue a grandmother. Does that make Ron a grandfather? Or is he a step grandparent? Or is there such a thing?

Intrigued by the relationships next door, I envision a time when Kristy is explaining who is whom to baby.

I slowly shake my head in disgust.

My husband wakes up, fluffs his pillow, and asks what we're having for breakfast. At the same time, I hear eight-year-old Julie bounding downstairs for the morning cartoons. I roll out of bed and head for the shower. After breakfast I load the dishwasher, wipe off the counters, and work on a sewing project I've started. Julie taps on the door.

"There's something I want to show you," she murmurs. Clearing a space, she lays down a piece of notebook paper folded in half like a greeting card. On the front is a crayoned rainbow. On the inside are large red letters:

Dear Kristy,
I'm happy you had a baby. Jessica is a pretty name.

Hmm, I muse. *Jessica. So it's a girl. . . .*

Underneath is the drawing of a smiling, toothless baby and the words "God Loves You." It's signed, *"Love from your next-door neighbor, Julie."*

After my daughter leaves the room, I lean on the sewing table, chin in hand, and think about this. Then I go looking for my daughter.

"Don't give it to her yet," I say. "Would you like to get a little gift, too?"

"Yeah, Mom!"

We drive to K-Mart where we buy a silly yellow duck wearing a blue hat. When we return home, Julie wraps the duck and tapes the card on top, and we take it next door. As we wait on the porch, I'm surprised that I never noticed the pretty welcome sign. But then, I've made no effort to become acquainted with Sue at all. She has so many family members, while I've been married to the same man for over fifteen years. I'm just unable to identify with Sue's kind of life.

When Sue answers the door—that is, I think it's Sue—I am embarrassed at having to introduce myself.

"I'm Karen, from next door. This is my daughter, Julie."

Sue, wearing her dark curly hair in a ponytail and dressed in jeans and a flannel shirt, looks quite normal. She smiles warmly and invites us in to see the baby. Kristy is on the couch, cuddling and kissing her precious bundle. Julie hands Kristy the duck and asks to hold Jessica, while I apologize.

"I'm sorry I haven't come over to meet you before now. Just busy. You know how it is."

Sue laughs and offers me a cup of coffee. I look around the room and am surprised at the cozy atmosphere. But what had I expected to see? Purple gremlins poking out of the corners, with a big sign that reads WEIRD FAMILY LIVES HERE? A basket of yellow daisies rests on a side table, and on the wall above it hangs a creatively arranged collection of photos. Pictures of Sue and Ron. Kristy and Todd. Chad. Scott. And I know that a space is reserved for Jessica.

Over coffee and a crescent roll, I learn more about Sue, and our woman talk turns to personal stuff—the kind where you feel so comfortable with someone you can tell her you hide candy bars in the linen closet.

"I never thought divorce would be a part of my life," Sue says. "We were married for ten years when my husband just up and left. Fell in love at the watercooler."

Ron, I learn, has been widowed for four years. "Breast cancer," Sue explains. "It was awfully hard on him." She gives a deep sigh.

"I don't know if it was the divorce or what, but Kristy's been a real handful lately. Now. . ." She motions to Kristy, who is fussing over the baby.

My throat begins to feel tight and funny, making it hard to swallow. This wasn't at all what I had imagined. Suddenly I don't like myself very much.

When it's time to leave, Sue and I plan to get together again. Julie skips home across the yard, unaware that her simple, nonjudgmental act has caused a major turnabout in my judgmental heart.

After going inside, curiosity makes me reach for my Bible to look up verses with "neighbor" in them. I stop at Proverbs 11:12: "A man who lacks judgment derides his neighbor, but a man of understanding holds his tongue."

"God Loves You," Julie had printed at the bottom of the card.

And He does, indeed. Sue. Ron. Kristy. Todd. Chad. Scott. Jessica. Me. People.

I go to the kitchen, get out the large blue bowl, and stir up a batch of chocolate chip cookies. Sometimes it's never too late to welcome people to the neighborhood.

When the World Became One
by Norka Blackman-Richards, Rosedale, New York

The United States was a long way from Panama City as my husband
and I dashed to the airport to return home to New York that day.
Before leaving my parents' house that morning, I saw the airplane
crash into one of the World Trade Center towers on television. But
we didn't grasp the impact of what we saw. We were too involved in
packing and saying good-bye. My mother dropped us off at the airport and went on to her job of teaching English at a prominent
high school.

We checked our luggage while hearing pieces of information:
"Terrorist attack on the United States." "Airports closed."
"Airplanes used as missiles." The atmosphere was tense as airport
security crowded the lobby. Bomb-squad units and dogs pushed
through the nervous crowd. I called my mother. Her voice was agi-
tated. "This is pandemonium! Students are crying and parents are
crowding into the classrooms and grabbing their children."

We were assured it was safe to board our flight. I started to
pray. "Dear Lord, if it is not Your will and our lives will be in
any type of danger, let our feet not leave Panama today." Then airport officials announced: "No one traveling to the United States

can leave today. There has been a terrorist attack on the United States, and air space is closed."

After waiting for hours for our suitcases, we returned to my parents' home. We watched the reports on TV in horror. Tears filled our eyes as we heard of the death totals.

We contacted a leader in our church. We had been assigned to the New York congregation in March 1999. Many members of our church worked in or near the Twin Towers. We learned that our sound technician, who worked in one of the towers, was missing. We felt powerless. It was disastrous that as the ministerial couple we could not be there to comfort his family and the congregation. How we longed to minister to our brothers and sisters and pray with them. We needed to get home. We felt that no one in Panama could understand our pain.

Soon we realized how wrong we were. America's pain had become the world's pain. These heinous crimes not only had touched one of the world's superpowers, but also had touched every human in some way. Friends, even strangers, called my parents' home to check on us and offer words of comfort. Although many of these people had never been to the United States, they felt our pain. Churches in Panama held prayer vigils for our church family and the American people. Memorials were erected throughout the city with roses, teddy bears, white sheets, handkerchiefs, notes, and Panamanian and American flags of all sizes. Schoolchildren and adults left testimony of their solidarity.

The world's outpouring of sympathy was overwhelming. We

cried as we learned of the memorials in diverse parts of the world. The poorest nations and the wealthiest superpowers had become one. The pain of the mothers, fathers, husbands, wives, and children became the pain of the world. The brave rescue workers on Ground Zero became the world's heroes. The energetic appeal of the U.S. president and Congress for the eradication of terrorism became the world's aim.

Perhaps more than any other historical event, September 11, 2001, will be remembered as the day the world became one, making a collective turn toward God as we prayed and mourned together.

TUSLOG Det 66

by Jacque E. Day, Chicago, Illinois

It was at TUSLOG Detachment, "Det" 66, where in 1964 at age nineteen, my father spent his first Christmas away from home. Det 66 housed the Signal Corps, which was in charge of long-range communications. My father, Private First Class Charles Day, worked as a cableman, laying cable from Turkey all the way to Ethiopia.

TUSLOG (The U.S. Logistics Operational Group), they were told, was the first line of defense against a Soviet attack, and instant communication over very long distances was essential to thwarting invasion efforts. And it was there, in the barracks of Det 66, that a little Turkish man of Islamic faith, who shined shoes for a living, gave one hundred lonely American boys a surprise Christmas gift that brought each of them to tears.

They didn't know him by name, but they came to count on him. Each day he greeted the American soldiers as they came off duty. He sat cross-legged in the entryway of the barracks with his shoe-shine kit, good-natured and relaxed. The American soldiers welcomed the small, inexpensive comfort afforded them by the little man who shined their regulation shoes each day—two pairs per man per day. He was perhaps forty-five years old, the same age as their fathers, and definitely too old to shine shoes, at least by American standards, but he worked deftly, making his way through two hundred pairs of shoes each night with the speed and skill of a true craftsman. Hours after he started, the little man would finish the last shoe, pack his kit, and head off for the bus stop. For his labors, each paid the little man the U.S. equivalent of twenty-five cents a week.

They liked him. His quiet, polite demeanor relaxed them, and his work made their lives easier. Each night as he made his way through the bunks, the soldiers made attempts to strike up conversation. He knew about as much English as they did Turkish, which wasn't much on either account, so they communicated mostly through hand gestures. But sometimes some understanding would seep through.

He lived in the capital city of Ankara. He had a wife and five children. He was Islamic. Two of his sons were about the same age as the soldiers, who were anywhere from seventeen to twenty-three. He rode the bus. It was a long ride that sometimes took three hours. Apparently the income he generated at the barracks must have been worth spending six hours a day riding a bus over a bumpy road.

On December 23, 1964, PFC Charles Day made his typical off-duty hike to the mess hall. For Christmas week, the army decided to treat the boys with generosity, which meant more white meat in the creamed turkey, bigger desserts, apple cider, and a few lights strewn around the mess hall. Still, it was less of a comfort and more a reminder of what they were missing at home. They ate the better than usual meal in solemn silence, all thinking the same thing. Most of them barely out of high school, all still closer to being boys than men, there they sat, two days away from Christmas, eight thousand miles away from home, wearing regulation work gear and eating from metal trays. The feeling wasn't just sadness or emptiness or loneliness. It was a combination of all those things. They quietly finished their meals and headed for the barracks.

At the barracks, they found their little Turkish shoe-shine man, seated cross-legged as always in the entryway. Next to him sat a decorated tree so small that it stood no higher than he sat. Under the tree were one hundred small wrapped gifts, one for each soldier. Not one man had been forgotten.

This poor, uneducated little man who shined shoes for a living had reached into their hearts and relieved the feelings that silenced them in the mess hall. How did he understand? How did he know? Perhaps as a father, he saw his own sons in each of them. This little man who traveled six hours a day to earn a fraction of their wages, who seemed to have nothing to give, had somehow managed to give them everything. And so these soldiers of TUS-LOG Det 66 wept openly as a poor Islamic shoe-shine man, whose name they didn't know, handed each of them a gift.

In a few weeks, my father was transferred and never returned to TUSLOG Det 66. But he never forgot the man who, perhaps without knowing it, gave a handful of lonely boys the most memorable Christmas of their lives. My father's five-foot, eight-inch frame towered over the tiny man. But to this day, close to forty years later, he swears that the little Turkish shoe-shine man was a very big man indeed.

Miracle on Mercer Street

by Carol Genengels, Seabeck, Washington

It was a balmy summer day with sunshine and gentle breezes.
Seagulls screamed and fluttered in the blue skies as our family
boarded the ferry bound for Seattle. We joined several church friends
aboard the vessel. Everyone was excited about going to Seattle
Center's opera house to see "Miracle on Azusa Street." A cast from
California was presenting the musical as an evangelical outreach.

After the ferry docked, our party walked to a waterfront restaurant.
Most of us ordered seafood, but five-year-old Ryan wanted a hamburger
and fries. He was too excited to eat more than a few bites.

After lunch we headed for the monorail that would zoom us to
Seattle Center. I grasped Ryan's hand as we trudged up steep hills. His
other fist clutched a doggie bag holding the remains of his lunch. We
heard a chorus of groans as we approached the monorail terminal. It
was closed for repairs. While some opted for taxis, the rest of us
decided to catch a city bus.

Our gang spread out as we boarded the crowded motor coach.
Ann, Ryan, and I found seats near the front of the bus. Ryan stared
at the bedraggled stranger sitting across the aisle from us. He hun-
grily eyed Ryan's doggie bag.

"Would you like a hamburger?" Ryan asked the man.

The stranger nodded and mumbled "thanks" as he reached for the bag. His smile revealed missing teeth. Ryan's blue eyes watched intently as the man wolfed down the burger and fries. He wiped his mouth on the back of his hand.

"What's your name, little boy?"

"Ryan. What's yours?"

"The name's George. Thanks for the burger."

"You're welcome," Ryan said.

George brushed stringy black hair away from his brown eyes. "Where are you all going on this fine day?"

Ryan told him we were on our way to see a play.

"Oh," he said before proudly announcing, "I'm an American Indian."

"Really!" I said, joining the conversation. "My friend, Ann, has Indian blood, too."

Ann engaged George in a discussion about their common roots. He gave his full attention, but most of his responses didn't make much sense.

We reached our destination, and our gang filed off the bus. My husband, Ted, caught up with Ryan and grasped his hand. George got off, too, and fell into step behind us. His disheveled clothes reeked of body odor and stale urine.

"So. . .you're going to a play?" George asked.

"Yes, we are," Ted said.

"How much does the play cost?"

"Nothing. It's free!" Ted responded.

"Can anyone go?" George inquired.

"Sure," Ted answered. "Would you like to come with us?"

George nodded. Ann and I exchanged glances as we joined the throngs of well-dressed people assembled in front of the posh opera house. Massive doors swung open, and we filed in. The splendid lobby impressed many, especially our guest. George stuck close to Ted as we made our way through the crowd. We were ushered down thick carpeting to the front of the theater. Our group settled in the first three rows. George had an aisle seat by Ted. Ryan and I sat on the other side of Ted. Ann settled in front of us.

Since we were early, we had plenty of free time before the play began. Ted did his best to ignore the rank odor as he treated George like an old friend. George began confiding in Ted, educating him about life on the streets. He confessed that he had "a bit of a drinking habit." George said he'd once been trapped in a fire that left his body covered with scars. He rolled up his shirtsleeves, revealing some of the disfiguring welts.

Ann turned around from time to time to offer breath mints. Ted thanked her as much as George did.

Before long the huge opera house was packed. We had the best seats in the house. The din of voices quieted as the orchestra began playing and the curtain opened. We were soon carried away to Azusa Street as talented singers and actors portrayed the story.

When it came time for the intermission, George left his seat abruptly. Ted went looking for him but couldn't find him in the crowded lobby. We were disappointed to think that George would miss the ending.

Shortly before the lights dimmed, George returned to his seat. His hair was slicked back, and he had washed his face and hands. Somewhere beneath the grimy exterior lived the soul of a ruggedly handsome man. I overheard George confide in Ted, "You know, my mother has been praying for me for years and years, always begging God to save me. I guess I gave her a pretty hard time in the past."

The lights faded and the music began. As the story progressed toward the climax, George repeatedly brushed tears from his eyes. He wasn't the only one.

The play ended with an altar call. Young and old alike streamed toward the stage to dedicate their lives to the Lord. George was at the head of the line.

We bid our new brother in Christ good-bye as we exited the grand opera house. George held his head a little higher as he slowly made his way down Mercer Street and disappeared into the crowd.

A Father's Love
by Michael T. Powers, Janesville, Wisconsin

Brian was a special education student at the small high school I attended. He was constantly searching for love and attention. It usually came for the wrong reasons, from students who wanted to have some "fun." He was the joke of the school and was "entertainment" for those who watched. Brian, who was looking for acceptance, didn't realize they were laughing at him, not with him.

One day, I couldn't take it anymore. I had enough of their game and told them to knock it off. "Aw, come on, Mike! We're just having fun. Who do you think you are, anyway?" The teasing didn't stop for long, but Brian latched on to me that day of my sophomore year. I had stuck up for him, and now he was my buddy. Thoughts of *What will people think of you if you are friends with Brian?* swirled in my head, but I forced them away as I realized that God wanted me to treat this young man as I would want to be treated.

Later that week I invited him over to my house after school to play video games. We sat there playing Intellivision (this was the '80s) and drinking Tang. Pretty soon he started asking me questions like, "Hey, Mike, where do you go to church?" I would politely answer his questions, then turn my concentration back to the video games. He kept asking me questions about God and why I was different from some of the kids at school.

Finally, my wonderfully perceptive girlfriend, Kristi, pulled me aside and said, "Michael, he needs to talk. How about you go down to your room where you can talk privately?" She had picked up on the cues better than I had.

As soon as we arrived in my room, Brian repeated, "Hey, Mike, how come you're not like some of the other kids at school?" I knew I needed to share with him the difference that God had made in my life. I got out my Bible and shared John 3:16 and some verses in Romans with him. I explained to him that God loved him just the way he was and that He sent Jesus down to earth to die on a cross for him. All the while, I did not know if he was comprehending anything I was telling him. When we were done, I asked Brian if he wanted to pray with me. He said he would like that.

We prayed together: "God, I know I am a sinner, and that even if I were the only person on earth, You still would have sent Your Son down to die on the cross for me and take my place. I accept the gift of salvation that You offer, and I ask that You come into my heart and take control. Thank You, Lord. Amen."

I looked at him and said, "Brian, if you meant those words you just prayed, where is Jesus right now?"

He pointed to his heart and said, "He is in here now."

Then he did something I will never forget as long as I live. Brian hugged the Bible to his chest and lay down on the bed, and tears flowed down his face. Brian was unearthly silent as the faucet behind his eyes let loose. Then he said to me, "Mike, the love that God has for me must be like the love a husband has for his wife." I was floored.

Here was someone who had trouble comprehending things in school but who now understood one of eternity's great truths. I knew that he understood what I had shared with him.

About a week later everything came into perspective for me. It was then that Brian really opened up to me. He explained that his dad had left him and his mom when he was five years old. Brian was standing on the porch the day his dad told him he was leaving. He told Brian he couldn't deal with having a son like him anymore; then he walked out of Brian's life and was never seen again. Brian told me that he had been looking for his dad ever since.

Now I knew why the tears kept flowing that day in my bedroom. His search was over. He found what he had been looking for since he was five years old—a father's love.

He would never again be alone.

Faith at Iwo Jima

by Nancy Cripe, Minneapolis, Minnesota

Sergeant Jack Starr went ashore with his Fifth Marine Division on the black ash beaches of Iwo Jima on February 19, 1945. The twenty-one thousand Japanese defenders holding the eighteen-square-mile sulfur island had gone into a labyrinth of caves. They waited until American troops had landed and piled their equipment on the beaches before pounding the Americans with artillery, rocket, and mortar fire.

Sergeant Starr and his comrades struggled over shifting and heavily mined sands toward garrisons in the rocky cliffs. The marines then began digging out the Japanese from sixteen miles of tunnels and fifteen hundred caves in hand-to-hand combat.

Five days into the battle, six marines raised the American flag atop Mount Suribachi. The now-famous photograph of the event won the Pulitzer prize and was fashioned into a Marine Corp monument. Three of the six flag-raisers died on Iwo Jima.

Acre for acre, this island was World War II's bloodiest battle. One in three of the seventy-five thousand marines who went ashore was killed or wounded. Only one thousand of the Japanese survived.

"I have thanked God daily for His watch care and guidance over me, and it's a miracle that I'm still alive," Starr wrote his family on March 12, three weeks into the campaign that was supposed to have lasted three days. "We have just come off the lines after eight days. This is the second time we have come back, and we're just hoping we don't have to go back up." But twenty-one-year-old Sergeant Starr went back up.

The Allies needed Iwo Jima's three airfields to have a strategic air base halfway between the U.S.–held Mariana Islands and the Japanese mainland, 650 miles away. Short-range fighter escorts protected the long-range bombers during air strikes on the Japanese home islands. But these fighters didn't have the range of the big bombers and needed a refueling station. Crippled B-29s hit by enemy fire also needed a base for emergency landings.

Starr was a Minnesotan, one of seven children. He had attended high school at Minnehaha Academy, a Christian school in Minneapolis. There his classmate John Pearson became his close friend. Starr, the class president, and Pearson, the salutatorian, graduated in 1941. Each joined the service soon afterward, Starr as a marine paratrooper and Pearson as a navigator with the army air force.

"It isn't the easiest thing to leave home, family, church, and friends, but we have a job to do, not only for our country but for our Lord, as well," Jack Starr wrote to his church. While in the South Pacific, he organized prayer meetings that grew from a handful of marines to large gatherings. "There is no greater privilege than helping a soul find peace in the

Almighty, and that has been my privilege," Jack wrote. "God's way is the best way. I made Him my Commanding Officer, and Jesus never fails."

Lieutenant John Pearson became navigator of the *Tamerlane*, a B-29 bomber. The crew nicknamed him "Deacon."

Being Christians in the military also brought Starr and Pearson challenges. On Christmas night 1944, a discouraged Jack Starr was "just going to give up; it seemed useless to try to tell the fellows about Christ because they just laughed at me." But then he prayed.

"About two minutes later, one of the boys called me outside. He said he could tell I had something he didn't have. He told me he wanted Jesus to come back into his life, so we prayed. I can't tell you how grand I felt inside. Helping that fellow turn back toward God was amazing. I could burst for joy to think that Jesus could work through me. Thank God, He can work through anyone who will let Him."

Sergeant Jack Starr went back up on the lines for a third time as the marines attacked Japanese defenses. Three days after writing his last letter home, Jack was killed in action on March 15, 1945. The news of his death reached home on Easter eve. "No matter what comes, my faith and trust are as solid as rock, and He will keep that which is committed unto Him," he had written his parents. "Remember, not 'good-bye,' just 'so long,' and God continue to bless our family as long as we stay true to Him."

The day after Starr's death, a B-29 returning from a bombing mission to Japan ran short of fuel. The plane was forced to land on Iwo Jima's Airfield No. 2, which was still under attack. The navigator who crawled out onto the runway was Lieutenant John Pearson.

John "Deacon" Pearson flew twenty-three B-29 missions, including a quartet that required emergency landings. After World War II, he married, raised five sons, and served for thirty years as a Lutheran pastor.

Sergeant Jack Starr was buried with thirteen thousand World War II comrades in the Punchbowl, the National Memorial Cemetery of the Pacific in Hawaii. Admiral Chester Nimitz, commander of the Pacific Fleet, said of the marines' thirty-six-day assault, "Among the Americans who served on Iwo Island, uncommon valor was a common virtue."

Jack Starr believed in valor and sacrifice. But more than that, he believed, "Greater love has no one than this, that he lay down his life for his friends" (John 15:13).

My Buddy Jules
by Paul Madison, Williamstown, New Jersey

I had only known Jules for about three months. He had already been working for a year at the luxurious high-rise apartment building on what is known as the Main Line of Philadelphia. Although he had spent most of his thirty-two years in poverty, which would harden most people, there was something kind about him. He was quick with a joke or something silly that would bring laughter to the rest of us on the maintenance staff.

He had this one special talent of driving us crazy with his singing at the most inappropriate times. We would be struggling with a repair job, and he would start his crooning. The trouble was that he would pick the only line from the song that he knew and sing it over and over again. After hearing this ten times in a two-minute stretch, someone would say, "If you sing that one more time, I'm gonna caulk your mouth shut," and Jules would say something to the effect of, "What, you don't like that song?" Most of us would just reply, "The song's okay, but you keep singing the same thing over and over. Can't you sing something else? You're driving me up the wall." Jules would clear his throat and ask, "How's 'bout this one?" And then he would sing the same lyrics yet again. We would just shake our heads and laugh.

The day that I will remember for the rest of my life as the working of the Lord, Jules and I were working on the fourth floor where the study room and our shop are located. The study room was for the many undergrads who lived in the building or for anyone who just wanted to get away and read the paper in peace. It included an area with all kinds of vending machines. As I walked past the study room, I saw a young fellow of about twelve who looked as though he was buying a soda. I continued toward the shop to get Jules because I needed his help.

As Jules and I approached the study room, I decided to get a drink. While I was putting money into the machine, I saw Jules's hand reach over toward one of the vending machines, grab something, and hurriedly put whatever it was into his pocket.

"Okay, pardner, what did you find?"

"Nothing, man. You can't find what you own."

"Wait a minute here. What are you talking about, Jules? What did you find?" Jules pulled out two crumpled-up twenty-dollar bills, and he was grinning from ear to ear.

Then I remembered the boy who had been near the machine only about five minutes earlier. "I think I know who that belongs to, Jules." The grin left Jules's face, replaced by a look of anger that I had never seen from him.

"Yeah, you know who it belongs to. Me! I found it, and it's mine now." Jules wadded up the money and stuffed it back into his pocket. I started to explain to him about the young guy I had seen a moment ago, but he cut me off. "Let me tell you something. I had my bike stolen from me this week. I used that bike 'cause I don't have a car or a license. I live in a shack where the roaches and the mice are threatening to call the Board of Health. So you think I'm worried about some rich kid who lives in this building getting his money back? I'm thirty-two years old, and I ain't got forty dollars to lose, let alone give it back to somebody I don't even know. So just forget it. It's mine now."

I was taken aback by this tirade. I hadn't seen such anger or bitterness from Jules in the time I thought us to be friends. We started to leave the room when in walked the young fellow I assumed had lost the money. He had an anxious look on his face when he asked, "Excuse me, but I lost some money in here. Did you see it?" Jules had a cold look on his face as he said, "No, we didn't see no money. You should be more careful." I caught Jules's eyes as we started to walk out the door.

Once we were out of earshot, I had to ask him, "Since you know who that money belongs to now, do you feel like the owner or do you feel like a thief?" We both looked back into the study room and watched as the young man tried in vain to look behind the machines. This time when we saw his face, he was wiping tears from his eyes.

Jules shrugged his shoulders and said, "Too bad for him."

Now I was angry as I walked away from Jules. Angry with someone whom I thought was a friend and angrier with myself for not doing the right thing. Jules surely would have lost his job if I had spoken up after he denied having the money. I looked at the half-filled paint cans and thought I would love to go over and knock them all over the shop. Just as I was about to sit down on a milk crate, our manager, Mike, walked in and said, "I've got to get ahold of Jules."

My heart jumped, fearing that the young man had put two and two together and come up with me or Jules as the culprit. "What do you want to see him for, Mike?"

Mike shook his head in disgust. "I want to see if that knucklehead wants one of those two bikes out on my patio."

Being the building manager, Mike lived on the premises and had two relatively new bikes that his kids never rode. "I just want to get rid of them before they get any more rust on them and they're worthless."

Well, I thought to myself, *how do you like that?* Jules takes some kid's money, then someone replaces the bike that was stolen from him. I wanted to tell Mike to give the bike to somebody more deserving when Jules appeared in the doorway. "Well, I hope you're happy."

"What do you mean, Jules?" I asked.

"I just hope you're happy. I gave that dumb kid his money back."

"What kid? What money?" Mike asked. I felt a moment of relief from my own guilt.

"Nothing, Mike. Jules found this kid's money, and he was teasing about not giving it back."

Mike just looked at Jules and said in mock anger, "I'm

giving you one of the bikes out on the balcony. But if you ever sing that stupid song again, I'm taking it back."

Jules looked at me and said, "Thanks, man."

"Thanks for what?"

"For telling Mike I needed a bike 'cause mine got stolen."

Before I could get the words out, Mike yelled at Jules. "He didn't tell me nothing about no bike. I saw that piece of junk you had when I took you home the other day and figured if anyone needed a bike, you did." Jules thanked Mike as Mike closed the door yelling, "Yeah, whatever."

I couldn't wait to find out what brought on the change of heart. "So what made you do it? Did that kid threaten you?"

Jules just smiled. "Nah. I just thought about my life and how hard it's been. I know He doesn't make deals, but I thought maybe if I did something nice for somebody, God would do something nice for me. And I just remembered how I felt when I went downstairs to get my bike and it was gone. Then I realized that there's a way to change the things in my life, and the start is changing myself. I also want to thank you for helping me."

"Thank me? For what?"

"You made me think of the Lord."

I was taken aback again. "I made you think of the Lord?"

"By you acting as my conscience, you made me remember the more important things. And keeping that money would have set me back. I've been doing a lot of prayin', and sometimes I think it's worthless. But I've come a long way in the last few months."

Jules went on to tell me that he had been hooked on drugs, and he was unreliable to his friends and family. He had started praying awhile back, and he had seen a change in his life, but it was slow and small.

As much as I wanted to take the credit, I realized that God had stepped in and answered Jules's prayers.

"Sorry, Jules. I'd like to take the credit, but I can't. There is something in you that deserves the credit. I think the sacrifice you made by giving that money back to help dry that kid's tears will be rewarded someday." I'd forgotten about the bike.

"Rewarded, huh? That bike is the first installment!" We both laughed and went to lunch.

That was six years ago. There is something special in Jules now, too. It is the light he brings whenever he is around. He gives praise to God every day. I only wish I could be half the person he has come to be. On that day six years ago, he taught this self-righteous person that giving, when you are in need yourself, is the way to all good things. And I guess that is what it's all about, isn't it? That is what Christ did for us. Christ was in need, and He still gave His very life for us. That's a lesson that should remind us daily how to give of ourselves.

Someone Else's Child

by Janice Thompson, Spring, Texas

She wasn't born our daughter, though it might have taken more than a quick glance to establish that fact. She had the same shiny chestnut hair, the same rosy complexion, and a sense of humor to rival that of each of our other three daughters. But she was born someone else's child.

We first met Betha when she was thirteen. She was a neighborhood kid, new to the youth group at church, and my kids had taken a liking to her. She wasn't exactly the kind of kid a parent would be drawn to immediately. In fact, she was plenty rough around the edges.

I often asked my daughters about Betha. Who was she? What were her parents like? Where, exactly, did she live? The fact that she kept showing up at our door, day after day, was a clear indication to me that all was not well at home. I hadn't met her parents and knew very little about this child who seemed determined to become one of mine. Who was this little waif, and why did she have such a desire to be with us? Why had she taken to calling me "Mom" and treating my own girls more like sisters than friends?

I got all the answers to my questions late one night. She had just returned home after spending a full day with us when our telephone rang. I answered to a tearful Betha, her voice laced with panic.

"Mom, my dad is. . .sick. Can you come and drive him to the hospital?" Of course I would drive her father to the hospital! I found my way to their house and watched as her dad, frail and thin, got into my car. He looked gravely ill. Betha climbed in the backseat, face pale.

As we made our way to the hospital, I learned, much to my shock, that he was suffering not from the stomach flu, as Betha had suggested, but from alcohol poisoning. He was beyond being "just drunk," and it was clear he had struggled with alcoholism for years.

I didn't know if it was the alcohol speaking or the fear of impending death, but this man, a complete stranger, began to speak to me as a friend, pouring out his heart to me. He told me of Betha's mother, who had left him when Betha was five years old, never to be seen or heard from again. He spoke of a faith in God that he clung to with trembling hand, despite his situation. He bragged about Betha, his precious little girl, who had walked hand in hand with him down this rocky road.

I peered into the rearview mirror at Betha's tear-stained face and suddenly understood everything. Her eyes sought mine in the mirror. They met with silent understanding. She needed me. She needed us.

This was not the first time Betha's father had been rushed to the hospital in critical condition that summer, nor would it be the last. His battle with the bottle would continue for quite some time beyond our initial meeting. Days turned into weeks, and weeks into months. All the while, Betha stayed with us. We prayed, as a family, that God would protect her father, heal him, and help him, but we also recognized that the decision to quit drinking had to be his.

It was a cool October evening when Betha's father came to us, asking the question we had known would eventually come. Could we keep Betha for a year so that he could enter a treatment facility? We happily agreed. He signed a power of attorney that same night, and Betha came to live with us—legally.

Sadly, her father checked himself out of that facility after only four months, hitting the bottle once again. He wandered from state to state looking for work, looking for peace. In a moment of desperation, he arrived at a Christian facility accustomed to dealing with men in his situation, and he checked himself in. He remains in their care to this day.

And Betha? She is a happy, well-adjusted fifteen-year-old, whose most current concern is whether or not she will get to drive soon. She has had to struggle through the difficulties that being the child of an alcoholic brings but is conquering them all in Jesus' name. She has committed her life to Christ and lives daily to please Him. She is completely "family" now, arguing and bickering appropriately just like our other girls. She has a laugh that could turn any frown upside down. All in all, she is pure delight.

Betha writes her daddy often, and he sends childhood photos, a signal that he is thinking of her and loves her. And when I overhear people talking about Betha, hear them discussing her "situation," I am reminded of how far we have all come together.

"She's someone else's child," I sometimes hear them whisper. I correct them quickly.

"No," I respond, looking them squarely in the eye. "She's our daughter, and God planned it that way."

Just Keep Up with Me
by Carlin Hertz, Fort Washington, Maryland

January 27, 1994, was no ordinary day for Alabama State University. It was a day the whole Hornet football team would never forget. This day would forever be etched in the minds of sixty-six young men. It would change many lives for good.

The day was cloudy and a bit chilly. It had rained all day, but the rain let up just in time for the football team's daily conditioning session on the track. The players hated running in the cold on a slippery track.

"Zo, I do not feel like running today," I said to my roommate as we both laced up our running shoes and headed outside. I threw on a thick black sweatshirt to keep warm. We listlessly trotted over to Hornet Stadium. Within minutes, a gang of tired and complaining football players all walked in unison toward the track. Puddles splashed on our legs, dampening our clothes. We ignored it. Our minds were focused on the eight laps we would have to run.

The conditioning coach greeted us with a sinister smile. "Good afternoon, ladies. Welcome to my house." He laughed as he rubbed his thick beard and blew his whistle to get our attention.

I was stretching my hamstrings, trying to loosen up, when Darnell walked over and asked me to help him stretch. I really didn't know him that well, but he was a teammate. Besides, I'd heard nothing but good things about him. He extended his long, muscular arm to help me off the ground. He smiled, and then he sat down on the wet grass.

Darnell was no ordinary football player. He was a slender six feet, six inches tall, 265 pounds of solid muscle. He had the biggest feet I had ever seen. His size would intimidate most men. But Darnell was different. Despite his massive frame, he was gentle—the nicest guy I had ever met. I didn't know much about God then, but I heard that Darnell was a Christian. He never messed around with girls. He always went to church. If you had a problem, you could go to him, and he would help you through it. Darnell was a good influence on us all.

"You ready to knock these laps out, Carlin?" he asked as I stretched his hamstrings for him.

"I guess," I replied.

"Well, just keep up with me, and I'll get you through," he said as he jumped up and smacked my hand. The coach blew his whistle, and we all started running on the track.

We had to run eight laps, and then we had to do some sprints. I didn't know how I was going to get through it, but I stayed close to Darnell, like he told me to do. His presence kept my mind off the laps.

We were coming on the last lap, and I was a few feet behind Darnell. His long strides covered so much ground that I knew my baby strides would never catch him. I was determined to catch him, though, so that I could brag about it later at dinner.

Darnell was running at a good pace, not looking tired, when all of a sudden, he just collapsed. He crashed to the ground. I thought he was just tired and had fallen out, but he didn't get up. We all stopped and ran over to where he lay.

The student trainer ran over and frantically tried to help him, but she didn't really know what to do. By now, we could see Darnell was fighting for his life. His fists were balled up tight, and he struggled to breathe. Finally, he just stopped. The trainer kept trying to talk to him, "Darnell, stay with me." In the distance, we could hear the blaring sounds of an ambulance siren.

By the time the ambulance got there, though, I think it was already too late. He just lay there as the paramedics tried to revive him. They placed him in the ambulance. We were told to go back to our rooms and wait for further instructions. We left the track in tears, hugging each other and praying, something many of us had never done. We were stunned.

A couple of us decided to go to the dining hall together instead of to the solitude of our rooms. As we sat down, a team-mate ran over to us. "Everybody needs to go to the meeting room now!" From the look on his face, I knew that Darnell was gone.

"Hey, Kenny," I asked, "is Darnell all right?"

Kenny just looked at me and broke down.

Without thinking, I threw the glass in my hand, sending glass flying everywhere. "No! He can't be gone!" They had to hold me because I couldn't control myself. People who didn't know what was going on looked at me like I was insane.

They told us Darnell had died of a massive heart attack. Apparently he had high blood pressure, but he hadn't been taking his medication. I didn't want to accept his death. He was just twenty-two years old. I had just talked to him. Yeah, I had been to funerals, but to witness somebody alive one minute and dead the next was spooky. I had talked to him only minutes before.

During this time, a stranger from Cleveland arrived on campus. He was a missionary and had come to Montgomery to set up Bible studies on the campus. Jeff befriended a lot of the football players at a time when we really needed him and what he had to say. Learning that we had just lost a teammate, he set up weekly Bible studies in the football dorm. Every Wednesday night the room where the Bible study was held was packed with football players searching for answers. Many of my teammates had been very close to Darnell, and we couldn't figure out why he would die like that.

Through God and the Bible, Jeff soothed a lot of our pain and suffering. He told us the truth, and he told us about salvation through Jesus Christ. A lot of football players were saved during those Bible studies. Jeff and I became good friends. He told me that when he left Cleveland he hadn't known what to expect. He said that God had told him to take nothing with him, get on a bus, and head to Montgomery. He came right at the time we needed to hear God's Word the most. It was no accident he was here.

The good thing about Darnell's death was that he went to

heaven. He was saved. The rest of us weren't, though. Any one of us could have died on the track that day. Where would we have ended up? Suppose Darnell had not died? Would a lot of those players have given their lives to Christ? I doubt it. Darnell's death was the wake-up call it took to bring our entire team to Christ.

The Cross on the Chalkboard
by Mary Ellen Gudeman, Fort Wayne, Indiana

To my relief, the bell rang. It was a sweltering hot and humid day. I sighed as I stuffed my teaching materials into my briefcase. How could I expect these Japanese students with so little understanding of the Bible to comprehend the message of the Cross in a language that was not their own?

As I turned to erase the chalkboard, I almost bumped into a student who was standing beside me. I apologized in Japanese to the lanky young man. Looking down, he shuffled his feet from side to side. I vaguely remembered his slipping into the back of the classroom halfway through the lesson.

By custom not daring to look into my face, he stammered, "Speak Japanese, okay?" I assured him it was okay.

"Can that man help me?" he asked as he pointed to the cross I was about to erase from the chalkboard.

"He most certainly can!" I replied.

"I have a problem in my heart," the student blurted out. "I would like to speak with you about Him." The young man's name was Tsuji-san. We made arrangements to meet the following Tuesday.

From Friday to Tuesday, I wondered if Tsuji-san would have the courage to show up for our meeting. But he came at the appointed time, and bit by bit he related his story to me.

He had come from the mountains of Fukui-ken. Not always able to express himself verbally, he had kept a diary. Then, before coming to Osaka to enter Kansai University, his mountain home had caught fire and had burned to the ground. The family had saved the Buddhist altar, but Tsuji-san's diary lay ruined in the ashes. So many thoughts and dreams had been recorded in that diary. Then his closest friend in high school took his own life when he failed the university entrance exam. Tsuji-san managed to pass the stiff exams to enter this choice university. But now, in spite of this accomplishment, a shadow had crept over his life.

The big city had held many charms that distracted him from his loneliness and despair. But they never filled the emptiness in his heart.

"But, Tsuji-san, there is a great God who has a wonderful plan for your life," I told him, wondering how I could communicate some hope to this dejected young man. "Tell me," I said, "why did you come only once to the Bible class on Fridays?"

"Well, to tell you the truth, I wasn't interested in the Bible," he replied. "But last Friday I decided to come to the final Bible class." He paused and then added with painful effort, "I decided to attend and then. . .and then take my life. But when you drew that cross on the chalkboard," he recalled, "you told us, 'You are loved by someone—someone who died on the cross for you. . . .' " His voice trailed off in a sob.

I sat there staring at him. Could it be that although he heard just a portion of the gospel for the first time, and in a foreign language, he really understood it? The message of the Cross—represented on the chalkboard that day—had spoken to Tsuji-san's heart.

Before he left that evening, Tsuji-san fully understood that God loved him, and he had placed his trust in Christ. Later he sent me a long letter. He wrote: "For the first time I know why I am living. Returning home tonight, I flung myself down on my futon and prayed for the first time, 'God, I'm sorry.' " He added, "My joy was so great I cried for over an hour."

During his college days, Tsuji-san attended our church in Osaka. His faith grew as he studied the Bible. He loved children and poured himself into teaching Sunday school. Later he led Bible studies for the youth group and also counseled at Bible camp in the summers. Tsuji-san often returned to his mountain home to share the message of the Cross with his mother. One day she also believed.

When he entered his junior year of college, I returned with him to Katsuyama-shi near his home. He wanted to visit his old high school and tell the students there about the Cross. The question was whether the school would permit it. In an unexpected gesture of welcome, the teacher told him he could say whatever he wished. I was amazed that a public school would permit such liberty in speaking. Tsuji-san related his friend's suicide and then his own search for meaning in life.

"Jesus died for you," he said as he drew the cross on the chalkboard and explained God's love to the students. I could almost hear him repeating the same Bible lesson I had taught in his university club. That evening a number of high school students, along with their teacher, attended the tiny village church!

After graduation from his university, Tsuji-san became engaged to Miyako-san, a young woman in the church in Osaka. He believed God wanted him to return to the mountains of Fukui-ken to live with his bride-to-be. They established a Christian home in Fukui-shi. Shortly after marrying, they invited their neighbors into their living room for a Bible study.

Over the years, I would occasionally meet Tsuji-san when he and his wife and children visited Osaka. On one particular visit when he was alone, he telephoned me.

"Do you still go to Kansai University for the Bible class?" he asked.

I told him I did.

He stammered, "I'd—I'd like to sit again in that classroom where you drew the cross on the chalkboard."

I remembered that hot, sultry day at Kansai University many years before when all but one of the students of the club had gone off to class. When the Cross is lifted up—wherever, whenever— even on a chalkboard, people will be drawn to Jesus, and the Good News will spread in any tongue.

Cyber Witness
by Cindy Appel, St. Louis, Missouri

Rubbing my burning eyes—sore from staring at the computer screen for too long, too late at night—I could hardly believe what slowly scrolled across the screen from almost an entire continent's expanse away: "Why do you believe the way you do?"

It was totally unexpected. I was a novice at "Web surfing." Recently I had stumbled upon a bulletin board system dedicated to writers and their problems. I had found it most illuminating and enjoyable. I would use it to see what new tidbits of information I could gather from others struggling to get their words into print. On this particular night, I noticed an announcement on the board's home page. It said that I could "chat live" with fellow authors in "real time" in a "chat room."

Hmm, this could be interesting, I said to myself, clicking on the underlined blue print and finding myself suddenly thrust into the unusual world of cyberspace communications. The people there were discussing all sorts of things—some literary related and some not—using chat room jargon that I did not yet understand.

One woman asked for input on how to publish her poetry and received helpful suggestions from only a handful of the dozen or so denizens of the electronic gathering. I typed a few encouraging words and received a thankful reply. My optimism and compassion for her plight must have stood out in stark contrast from the rest of the crowd's responses. I soon discovered myself involved in a conversation with another chat room member with more serious undertones: "I am a loner. I don't feel as if I will ever be anything but lonely. . . ."

I was surprised by the plaintive plea for help. The faceless world of cyberspace contains real people after all—individuals who feel alone and unloved. In the anonymous realm of the electronic age, I had found a human being who desperately needed to know the love of the Lord.

In simple terms I shared my Christian faith across the World Wide Web with this one searching person. *This person whose face, name, and heart can be known only by God,* I thought. It wasn't a simple task. Others interjected their comments into the discussion—sometimes helpful, sometimes frivolous, and sometimes quite cynical. I kept right on typing. I gave my testimony to the power and love of Christ that I had seen throughout my life and in others' lives.

The hour grew later, my eyes wearier, and my hands tired. Soon my "cyber friend" and I were forced to call it a night. I could only pray that the seed that I had planted might take root and grow, eventually to blossom into faith within the life of this one individual.

My pastor has exhorted our congregation many times to

always be prepared to give witness, because all Christians are witnesses to the glory of our risen Lord. For some reason I had never imagined that my faith would be questioned or challenged in anything other than a face-to-face exchange. I would have immediate feedback—no twenty-second lags between mainframe computers on the Internet, no mistaking the impact of my words, for I could visually gauge the other's reaction.

Certainly, typed words on a computer screen couldn't have the same effect on a person as the spoken word—could they? Perhaps they can. In the twenty-first century, Christians should stand ready to follow Peter's instructions. He told those early believers to "always be prepared to give an answer" no matter when, where, or how the answer is needed. As you sit at your terminal and "talk" with your friends, loved ones, or even strangers, remember to "be prepared."

Jesus Christ is Lord and Savior for all time and through all ages. He abides with us even today—even in the cold complexity of the computer-dominated domain in which many of us reside. Perhaps because of that, the warmth of His love and forgiveness is needed now more than ever.

Nicholas
by Susan Farr Fahncke, Kaysville, Utah

My son Nicholas has always had a soft heart. It's the thing I love best about him. At thirteen, he is now struggling with the "macho" role society expects of him. I am proud that he has remained a compassionate and kind person even though the teenage years have struck. One such moment of pride was when he decided to give Christmas to a family in our neighborhood.

Chad and Derek are two boys who attend Nick's junior high. Junior high is painful enough for anyone, but for Chad and Derek, it was a daily nightmare. Living alone with their mother, they were the smallest boys in junior high. They wore the same worn, outdated clothes to school every day and were picked on constantly. Their mother is a loving, hardworking woman, but as most single moms know, there is rarely enough money left over for new clothes.

My son has always been sensitive to the pain of others. What most teenage kids wouldn't even have noticed, Nick immediately understood as embarrassment and pain lived out daily. Chad and Derek quickly became the subject of Nick's prayers and worries. He appointed himself their secret protector.

Every year at Christmastime, we select a family for whom we are

"Secret Santa." Last Christmas we had a family meeting and a vote for who would be the best candidate. The majority of our family voted for a disabled friend of ours who also happened to be a single mom with two teenagers. But Nick resolutely stuck to his decision to help the Williams boys. Not wanting to squelch my son's desire to make a difference in the life of someone else, I hesitated. I knew how important this family was to him. My husband and I conferred. We would be Secret Santa for both families.

Nicholas's eyes lit up. His thirteen-year-old grin made my heart soar. How many mothers were blessed with a teenage angel? Seeing the kindness in my child's soul brought tears to my eyes. I knew what a rarity he was.

It is our tradition to provide the makings of a Christmas dinner, as well as carefully selected gifts for our "Secret Santa" family each year. Without a doubt, Nick knew that we needed to buy the boys clothes. And they couldn't be just any clothes. They had to be "cool"; they had to be "in" clothes. Nick was determined to give Chad and Derek clothes that would stop the taunting and make them feel good about what they wore to school every day.

To many of us, this is a trivial, worldly thing, but when you are a young teenager, it is everything. Whether he realized it or not, Nick wanted to give them self-esteem, a chance to fit in. Quite a gift for a thirteen-year-old.

As we spent endless hours looking for just the right outfits for both boys, I concentrated on their mother. Having once been a single mom, I remembered the days of my own single motherhood. Every little bit of "extra" went to my children's needs. It had probably been a long time since she had done anything nice for herself.

Abandoning the kids to the boys' clothing department, I took a quick detour to the bath aisle. Smiling to myself, I selected a luxurious bath basket, filled to the brim with bubbles, soaps, lotions, and all kinds of "take me away" things that only a mom can truly appreciate. I found myself getting into the spirit of Nicholas's gift. I looked at clothes, makeup, jewelry, books. . . I finally selected a book of uplifting stories for mothers and a box of truffles. Delighted with myself, I couldn't wait to show everyone else what I had done. The spirit of Christmas filled my heart and overflowed into a joyous, childlike feeling of giddiness.

Returning to my children, I found they had finally settled on several articles of clothing that my son thought were "in." Judging the boys' sizes was difficult, but we did our best. Nick suddenly remembered that the boys wore only old, worn coats to school. Utah winters make good gloves a must. We chose the thickest, warmest, "coolest" gloves in the store, and I didn't even look at the price tag! We were all grinning with the sheer joy of giving.

We added a good family video and two great books, then put the Christmas dinner together. A fat turkey, all the trimmings, dessert, and candy for the boys went into the cart. We couldn't wait to deliver our packages and picture the looks on Derek's and Chad's faces. I secretly hoped their mother had as much fun opening her gifts as I had shopping for her.

Our cart overflowing, we headed for the checkout line. At first worried about spending too much, I was now filled with a great sense of peace. I knew that my husband wouldn't mind and that as blessed as we were, we ought to share those blessings with others. Standing in line, the thought kept coming back to me that money would be a much-appreciated gift. Maybe there was something this family really needed that I didn't know about. Next to the counter, there were store gift cards on a rack. I carefully looked at the amounts and said a quick prayer for guidance. I reached for the fifty-dollar gift card, but my hand picked up the one-hundred-dollar card. Praying again, I knew this was right and laid it on top of my purchases. I made a quick call to my husband to make sure this was not too much, and he surprised me with his assurance to go ahead.

I looked at Nicholas as his eyes fell on the gift card and laughed as he wheeled around in shock. "Is that for them?" he asked me. I nodded, and my eyes filled with tears as he threw his arms around me and thanked me as if the gift were for him. What an amazing kid I have.

That night we wrapped the presents and delivered the huge box to the family's doorstep. Nick rang the bell, and we all ran giggling down the street. The feeling of joy stayed with us long past that night. And it returned the day school resumed. Nick ran all the way home from school to tell me Derek and Chad wore their new clothes to school. They fit, and boy, did they look cool!

The planning and executing of our "Secret Santa" was the greatest gift our family got that Christmas, and I saw a side to my son that would make any mother weep. Teenage angels are hard to find these days, and I am so blessed that God placed one under our roof.

The Smiles of Children

by Jennifer Bottke, Lake City, Minnesota

At age nineteen, I went to southern India to learn about life—to experience, to grow, to change. God gave me the opportunity to do all those things on a three-week field visit I made to a little temple town called Tirupathi. I lived at a small residential school for the children of women who were forced into prostitution at the local temples.

Without this school, the children—especially the girls—would have been left to suffer the same fate as their mothers. I was horrified upon my arrival. The school was located in the middle of an enormous slum, surrounded by poverty, hunger, and sadness. Fear of the unknown overcame me. It lurked everywhere. I did the only two things I could think of. I prayed for strength and healing and threw myself into the children's daily lives.

I grew attached to those children. I didn't want to leave them when my time was up—a sharp contrast to my initial feelings. At first I dreaded my stay because I didn't have the "creature comforts" I was used to—running water, a bed, and a bathroom. But my departure date came all too soon. I wanted to stay and somehow watch over those children, to protect them from the cruelties of life, like the poverty that was sure to grip them outside their safe little school.

After we had taken a group picture on my last day, they all swarmed around me, pulling me down into them. I suddenly had a million little hands touching me and a million little mouths kissing my cheeks.

Some of the children had come down with a nasty fever. Little Mamatha was hot and still as she sat on my lap for the longest time that night. Her big brown eyes stared up into mine, telling more than words ever could have explained. I went into the infirmary to say good-bye to Madevi, a girl at the school who was my age. She was sleeping when I crept in to see her. I knelt down on the floor beside her as she rolled over to see me. She opened her eyes and managed a smile through her tears. I smiled back through mine as I grabbed her hand. She kissed my hand and went back to sleep.

Why did these children get dealt such a hard life when my life of privilege was granted to me so easily? I wondered. *I don't deserve my privileges any more than they deserve their constant hardships.*

The most amazing thing about my precious time with them came when I looked into their happy eyes and returned their bright, sunny smiles. I shared their joy, not sadness; their thankfulness for what they had, not their desperate need for money or food; their happiness that they were given this limited opportunity, not their misery at being left behind.

God gave me the chance to experience what I had never known or even dreamed—a chance to understand something completely foreign to me. Through each of these children, God showed me that to fear the unknown, to recoil from the hardships of life, would be to miss out on the greatest gifts He has to share. The simple truth in that lesson has changed my life forever.

Twinkle, Twinkle, Little Star

by Jeanne Zornes, Wenatchee, Washington

He wasn't someone who'd climb the executive ladder, this man I'll call "Ralph." He ran the shipping department of a small company where I worked one year. Built like a bear, his searching eyes almost hidden behind thick-lensed glasses, he'd put in his hours in a sunless room piled with boxes. Then, his day done, he'd catch a bus home.

I already knew Ralph was a Christian. Somehow he learned I played the violin. Maybe the subject came up in the company's attic lunchroom, as we sat at cast-off tangerine café tables and visited over peanut butter sandwiches and vacuum bottles of soup.

"My daughter wants to learn violin," he said. "There's one we could buy, but we don't have enough money for it." When he named the price he could afford, I knew it would buy only a no-frills student violin.

I played a student violin, too. I loved playing violin and studied it through college. Though music didn't become a vocation, I still played in small orchestras, at church, at meetings, even for my grandmother in a nursing home. I knew the positive dimension music brought to my life. I wanted that for Ralph's family.

But Ralph's problem with stretching a paycheck was also mine.

Single and thirty years old, I'd just finished two years as a missionary and had used up my savings to attend a year of Bible college. Now I was saving for graduate school. What could I do, when I didn't earn much above minimum wage?

When Thanksgiving came, I sensed giddiness among other employees as the finance officer passed out checks. I opened my pay envelope and found my employer's Christmas bonus.

Give it to Ralph, an insistent inner voice said.

But, Lord, I hardly know him, I protested. *You know how much I need to save for college. Every bit helps.*

Give it to Ralph.

God had been working in my heart over the past few years. Living on so little had caused me to pay closer attention to scriptures that talked about the poor. I had come to understand that God didn't see me as "poor" but rather as one through whom He could bless another.

I was surprised at the joy that replaced my anxiety as I wrote a check equal to the bonus and put it in a card I left on Ralph's workbench. "Please use this toward your daughter's violin," my note said.

A few months later Ralph's family invited me for dinner and a "concert." Three excited children clung to me as I entered their little home with its tired furniture. His wife, her hands knobbed with arthritis, served chicken on mismatched plates. His oldest daughter provided the after-dinner concert on her little violin, playing "Twinkle, Twinkle, Little Star."

I never missed that money. I still had enough for graduate school and for other times God prompted me to give to someone in need. "Cast your bread upon the waters," says Ecclesiastes 11:1. I could only cast crumbs on a vast ocean, but each time I did, I experienced quiet joy in simply obeying God.

Twenty years passed. I married, and we had two children. I passed on my love of music by enrolling both children in the school orchestra program. I listened proudly as they learned to play on used violins, advancing from "Twinkle, Twinkle, Little Star" to Bach and Beethoven. My husband's salary as a teacher wasn't extravagant, but it was sufficient for our needs. God allowed me to supplement our income with an at-home business involving a computer. But after ten years that computer was outdated.

The hope of replacing my computer was ended when a drunk driver plowed into our car as we returned home from a weekend away. My husband's last-second swerve to the ditch spared us a head-on collision and possibly our lives, but the side impact shot glass across our son's face, breaking teeth and pocking his face with wounds. Insurance wouldn't cover all the medical expenses. The next months were a challenge.

A year later I took my son in for his final plastic surgery to minimize his scars. The appointment meant not being able to see a Christian friend who was in town on business. I'd helped him a couple years earlier with a project that had proven very successful for him.

The next day my husband insisted on taking me out to

lunch. Eating out wasn't a high-priority budget item for us, but he had a two-for-one coupon.

"You've made some great friends in your work," my husband remarked as we poked chopsticks into our stir-fry. His remark veiled a secret to which I was not privy. "Let's stop by a computer store on the way home," my husband said as we paid for the meal.

"Let's not," I said. "I can't buy one."

I steamed as he pulled me into a local computer store and started browsing. Still ignoring my pleas to go home, my husband went to find a salesman. Both of them smiled at me.

"A friend of yours was here yesterday," the salesman said, showing me the friend's business card. And then pointing to a pile of boxes, he said, "He bought this for you. You're supposed to take it home and enjoy it."

I started shaking and crying as my husband revealed how this friend had called while I was at the hospital with our son. My friend said he was obeying a nudge from God by buying a computer system for me. I couldn't believe that someone would do this for me. I cried all the way home.

As I started unpacking the computer and figuring out all its plug-ins, the last part of the verse from Ecclesiastes came back to me: "Cast your bread upon the waters, for after many days you will find it again."

I had never expected to see that "bread" again, but "after many days," God, the greatest giver of all, had chosen to wash it back ashore in the shape of a computer. I smiled as I thanked Him.

Smiley
by Karen Garrison, Steubenville, Ohio

Lily Sturgeon changed my life. She was eighty-seven years old when I first met her, and I was a prima donna at the self-centered age of seventeen. She was a resident at the convalescent home I'd been volunteering at to better my final Health Assistant grade.

For weeks I had grumbled to my boyfriend about having to tend to people "for free." "After all," I told him, "every penny could've gone toward our 'after-graduation' celebration in New York." He heartily agreed.

And even worse, I soon realized, were the bright yellow uniforms my classmates and I were required to wear. On our first day at the geriatric center, the registered nurses took one look at our sunshiny apparel and nicknamed us "The Yellow Birds."

During my scheduled days, I complained to other yellow birds about how changing bedpans and soiled linen and spoon-feeding pureed foods to mumbling mouths were not things any teenager should have to do.

A tedious month passed; then I met Lily. I was given a tray of food and sent to her room. Her bright blue eyes appraised me as I entered, and I soon became very aware of the kindness behind them.

After a few minutes of talking with her, I realized why I hadn't noticed Lily before even though I had been past her room numerous times. Lily, unlike so many of the other residents, was soft-spoken and undemanding. From my first day at the geriatric center, I had learned that the staff had their favorite patients. Usually the favorites were ones who stuck out in some characteristic way. From joke-tellers to singers, the louder and more rambunctious the patient, the more attention he or she received.

Something inside of me immediately liked Lily, and strangely, I even began to enjoy our talks during my visits to her room. It didn't take long to realize that Lily's genuine kindness stemmed from her relationship with God.

"Come here," she said, smiling at me one rainy afternoon. "Sit down. I have something to show you." She lifted a small photo album and began to turn the pages. "This was my Albert. See him there? Such a handsome man." Her voice softened even more as she pointed to a pretty little girl sitting on top of a fence. "And that was our darling Emmy when she was eight years old."

A drop of wetness splattered on the plastic cover, and I quickly turned to Lily. Her eyes were filled with tears. "What is it?" I whispered, covering her hand with my own.

She didn't answer right away, but as Lily turned the pages, I noticed that Emmy was not in any other photographs. "She died from cancer that year," Lily told me. "She'd been in and out of hospitals most of her life, but that year Jesus took her home."

"I'm so sorry," I said, disturbed that God would take away this beautiful woman's daughter. "I don't understand why He let her die. You're such a true follower of His," I said.

"It's okay." She smiled slightly, meeting my eyes. "God has a plan for every life, Karen. We need to open our hearts to Him regardless of whether we understand His ways or not. Only then can we find true peace." She turned to the last page. Inside the worn album was one more picture of a middle-aged Lily standing on tiptoes and kissing a clown's cheek.

"That's my Albert." She laughed, recalling happy memories. "After Emmy died, we decided to do something to help the children at the hospitals. We'd been so disturbed by the dismal surroundings while Emmy was hospitalized." Lily went on to explain how Albert decided to become "Smiley the Clown."

"Emmy was always smiling," she recalled. "Even in the worst of times. So I scraped together what fabric I could find and sewed this costume for Albert." She clasped her hands in joy. "The children loved it! Every weekend we'd volunteer at the hospitals to bring smiles and gifts to the children."

"But you were poor; how'd you manage that?" I asked in amazement.

"Well," she said and grinned, meeting my eyes, "smiles are free, and the gifts weren't anything fancy."

She shut the album and leaned back against her pillows. "Sometimes the local bakers would donate goodies, or when we were really hurting for money, we'd take a litter of pups from our farm. The children loved petting them. After Albert died, I noticed how faded and worn-out the costume actually was, and so I rented one and dressed as Smiley until about ten years ago, when I had my first heart attack."

When I left Lily's room that day, I couldn't think of anything but how generous she and Albert had been to children who weren't their own.

Graduation day neared, and on my last day of volunteer services at the ward, I hurried to Lily's room. She was asleep, curled into a fetal position from stomach discomfort. I stroked her brow, worrying about who would care for her the way I did. Lily didn't have any other surviving family members, and most of the staff neglected her except for her basic needs, which were met with polite abruptness. At times I wanted to shout Lily's virtues to them, but she'd stop me, reminding me that the good things she'd done in life were done without thoughts of self.

"Besides," she would say, "doesn't the good Lord tell us to store our treasures in heaven and not on this earth?"

Lily must've sensed my inner torment above her bed that day, for she opened her eyes and touched my hand. "What is it, dear?" she asked, her voice concerned and laced with pain.

"I'll be back in two weeks," I told her, explaining about my high school graduation. "And then I'll visit you every day. I promise."

She sighed and squeezed my fingers. "I can't wait for you to tell me all about it."

Two weeks later to the day, I rushed back to the center,

bubbly with excitement and eager to share with Lily the news of my graduation events. With a bouquet of lilies in my hand, I stepped into her clean, neat, unoccupied room. The bed was made, and as I searched for an answer to Lily's whereabouts, my heart already knew the answer. I threw the flowers on the bed and wept.

A nurse gently touched my shoulder. "Were you one of the yellow birds?" she asked. "Is your name Karen?" I nodded, and she handed me a gift-wrapped box. "Lily wanted you to have this. We've had it since she died, because we didn't know how to get in touch with you."

It was her photo album. Written on the inside cover was Jeremiah 29:11: " 'For I know the plans I have for you,' declares the LORD, 'plans to prosper you and not to harm you, plans to give you hope and a future.' " I clutched it to my chest and departed.

Three weeks later my horrified boyfriend stood before me. "You can't be serious," he said, starting to pace back and forth. "You look ridiculous." We were in my bedroom, and as I tried to view myself in the mirror, he blocked my reflection. "You can't be serious," he repeated. "How in the world did you pay for that thing, anyway?"

"With my graduation money."

"Your what?" he exclaimed, shaking his head. "You spent the money we were going to New York with on that?"

"Yep," I replied, stringing on my rubber nose. "Life is more about giving than receiving."

"This is just great," he muttered, helping me tie the back of the costume. "And what am I supposed to tell someone when they ask me my girlfriend's name? That it's Bozo?"

I looked at my watch. I needed to hurry if I wanted to make it on time to the children's hospital. "Nope," I answered, kissing him quickly on the cheek.

"Tell them it's Smiley. Smiley the Clown!"

Angel of Kindness
by Linda Knight, Woodslee, Ontario

It was only a hug, a seemingly insignificant hug, and yet its gentle power helped to make a miracle happen.

She was new to our church. All I did was counsel her for a few brief moments after an altar call. She had been living in Canada for three years now, having escaped an abusive relationship in South Africa. I remember commenting on the beauty of her accent as we spoke that day. She told me of her escape from her homeland. At the airport, friends and neighbors had rallied around her, shielding her and her children from her outraged husband and the local police as they tried to stop her from boarding the plane to freedom.

I gave her a Bible and my phone number. I told her if she ever needed to talk to give me a call. That was when I hugged her. And then we parted company.

Three weeks later, the call came. At the first sound of my voice, she hung up. But she said something nudged her to try again. Thank heaven she did. She was beside herself with worry and grief. Her seventeen-year-old special needs son couldn't handle the cultural differences between his homeland and his adopted country, or the taunts and ridicule of classmates. Her own life since coming to Canada had been equally challenging. Thoughts of suicide began to occupy her mind, increasing daily. She was frightened of what she might do.

Then she remembered our encounter. She told me how much that hug had meant to her. The warmth of that touch had felt to her like Jesus assuring her that everything would be all right in time. It had planted a hope in her that she'd never experienced before. We talked for a long, long time that night. It was the beginning of a lovely friendship.

One day she phoned to say she had a gift she wanted to give me. There was a catch to the gift, though. I had to promise to give it away. My curiosity was piqued, and I waited eagerly for her to arrive.

She gave me a beautiful china angel. Its arms were outstretched, and it held a tiny dove in its right hand. It was, she told me, the Angel of Kindness, given in appreciation of random acts of kindness. It had been given to her some time ago by a person she had once helped. She said my hug and phone number had, quite literally, saved her life, and now the Angel of Kindness was mine for the moment. When I experienced a random act of kindness in my life, it would be time for the angel to take flight again.

No one is sure where the angel originated, but we know where it's going—from one act of kindness to another. We never know when the Lord will use us. Sometimes we don't even see the way He uses us, especially through random acts of kindness. Yet a simple act may be the glue that holds a life together. And it could be something as simple as a hug.

The Ivory Quill
by Darlyn Bush, Abbeville, Louisiana

Some adventures in life stay in your memory always. That day in the spring of 1923, in New Orleans, Louisiana, was one such day.

I was twenty-one and depressed beyond measure. With the *clip-clop* of horse-drawn carriages along the cobblestone streets following me down the sidewalk to Jackson Square, I felt as if everyone had a purpose for being except me.

I sat on a park bench quietly praying that God would send me a sign, something that would give a glimmer of hope to my invading disenchantment with life. Tears surfaced as I glanced up at the towering steeple of Saint Louis Cathedral. *Lord, please help me to understand my path to happiness,* I silently prayed.

As the last of my plea took flight with the spring breeze, a beautiful white dove perched on a bush in front of me. And just as suddenly as it had come, it flew across the square. My tear-filled eyes followed its course toward another park bench where it landed at the feet of an old gentleman sitting all alone. He had been feeding the pigeons the last of his sandwich. The last of his crumbs were thrown to the newcomer—the dove.

His clothes were rumpled and tattered, and his eyes revealed much loneliness. Something moved me to go and join this old soul. As I walked across the park, I stopped to buy two cups of coffee and some French beignets for the two of us. His joy at having someone to talk to and the merriment portrayed on his face after sipping his coffee and nibbling his sweets were more than enough thanks for me.

Before long he was talking at length and with great pride about the memories of his past, mostly as a Civil War soldier. He told of how his younger brother had fought for the other side and been killed by a Southern soldier from his own troop. He told of the cannons' thunderous roar as they lit the skies of twilight. And he shared stories of how the soldiers, most of whom were wounded, marched wearily across fields of dead bodies. Food and water were in short supply, and dysentery plagued the exhausted soldiers.

His pride, of course, was understandable—he was a proud veteran. But his obvious love and joy over mentioning these matters baffled me greatly. Maybe this was the only time that he ever remembered himself being needed or having a purpose in his life. It was soon obvious there was no one left who cared anything about him. He lived in a long-ago past, virtually oblivious to his current state.

Yet he never complained of his present plight. He was without socks to protect his feet from the ground that rubbed his flesh raw where the holes in his shoes were. He had no home, just a cardboard box to sleep in. Neither did he complain of his tattered clothes and lack of food—no, not this soldier of war. He was merely grateful for every day that he was able to make his way to the park to sit and feed his feathered friends.

How ashamed I became. Compared to his present circumstances, my life was bountiful. I had food in my pantry, a comfortable bed to sleep in, and good clean clothes on my back. I had friends who loved and cared about me. I now understood that I had my whole life ahead of me and realized that the things we might want are not always the things we really need.

This courageous old soul had instilled in me faith, insight, and enough determination to see life through—no matter what the odds might be. I, in turn, felt the glory of being responsible for the twinkle in his eyes and the contented smile on his lips.

I bowed my head in prayer, thanking God for bringing this gentle soul to my rescue. I made a decision at that moment to invite the old soldier home for dinner. As I raised my head to talk to him, I found he had gone. The dove also had disappeared. I looked in every direction but could not find them.

Suddenly, something on the bench where he had sat captured my eye. I reached down and lifted a white feather that was left in his place. *How peculiar,* I thought as I studied the ivory quill. The dove had never perched on the bench, yet its plume lay next to me.

I returned to Jackson Square for months on end trying to find that gentle soldier. I finally gave up the search when a white dove landed at my feet. I knew in my heart that I would never see the old man again.

I have kept that treasured feather throughout the years between the pages of my Bible. In my darkest hours, I have removed that ivory quill and recalled the finding of it. It never fails to bring me hope and joy.

Today is December 13, 1987. It is my seventy-fifth birthday. My oldest great-granddaughter, Amanda, is coming to visit me. She, too, is filled with despair. It is time to pass on the ivory quill and the old soldier's story with it.

So my precious Amanda and I will sit this afternoon, enjoying a cup of tea, and I will tell her of the tale that so long ago filled my life with hope and joy. I know in my heart that afterward Amanda will always love and remember this old, gentle soul—just as I have remembered him so well. And it will bring her hope and joy throughout her life until she, too, passes it on.

Project Founder

About the God Allows U-Turns Project Founder

Allison Gappa Bottke lives in southern Minnesota on a twenty-five-acre hobby farm with her entrepreneur husband, Kevin. She is a relatively "new" Christian, coming to the fold in 1989 as a result of a dramatic life "U-turn." The driving force behind the God Allows U-Turns Project, she has a growing passion to share with others the healing and hope offered by the Lord Jesus Christ. Allison has a wonderful ability to inspire and encourage audiences with her down-to-earth speaking style as she relates her personal testimony of how God orchestrated a dramatic U-turn in her life. Lovingly dubbed "The U-Turns Poster Girl," you can find out more about Allison by visiting www.godallowsuturns.com.

About the Contributors

Cindy Appel is an online columnist, novelist, freelance writer, manuscript evaluator, wife, and mother. Her articles, book reviews, and inspirational essays have appeared in more than twenty-five publications.

Norka Blackman-Richards lives in New York with her minister husband. She teaches writing and English as a second language and writes a weekly devotional. A pastor's child, Norka grew up in Latin America, Europe, and the Caribbean and values this experience as "priceless."

Jennifer Bottke lives in Minnesota where she is studying to become a registered nurse. With a passion for ministry to children, Jennifer looks forward to returning to third world countries where she can share Christ's love.

Darlyn Bush of Abbeyville, Louisiana, is a latecomer to the literary world, who, in spite of the dire warnings from professionals, has pursued her passion. She is thankful to God for the joy that her writing has given to both her and her readers.

Nancy Cripe lives in Minneapolis, Minnesota, with her husband, Brian, and children, Jonathan and Elizabeth. She likes to weave stories by drawing on her years of teaching science, traveling, and making friends from all over.

Jacque E. Day lives in Chicago, Illinois. Her work appears in various newspapers and small presses, and she holds the Linda Haldeman Award for Fiction. She is also a producer for the Discovery Health Channel series *Chicago's Lifeline*.

Sara A. (Candy) DuBose is a public speaker and author. Her specialties include humor, nostalgia, and God's work in unexpected places. Sara's novels, *Where Hearts Live* and *Where Love Grows,* are available on-line or through bookstores. For speaking engagements or autographed books contact: Hearts, 3739 Pine Cove, Montgomery, AL 36116, or phone: 334-284-2010.

Susan Farr Fahncke of Kaysville, Utah, is a freelance writer and runs her own Web site. She has had stories published in numerous books and magazines.

Rusty Fischer is a popular Christian author whose stories have appeared in *Chicken Soup for the Soul* and *Cup of Comfort.* Rusty is a freelance writer who enjoys working at home—mostly because it allows him to spend more time with his beautiful wife, Martha.

Karen Garrison is an award-winning writer specializing in stories that encourage faith. She is a wife and mother of two.

Carol Genengels and her husband have three children and five grandsons. They live on scenic Hood Canal near Seattle. She is the cofounder/director of A Woman's Touch Ministry and enjoys traveling, teaching, and prayer.

Mary Ellen Gudeman was born on a farm in Indiana. She attended Fort Wayne Bible College and served twenty-six years in Japan with the TEAM organization. She volunteers at a local refugee outreach ministry.

Patty Smith Hall served as a board member of the American Christian Romance Writers and is a novelist. She lives in Hiram, Georgia, with her husband, Dan, and their daughters, Jennifer and Carly.

Carlin Hertz lives in Fort Washington, Maryland. He is married to Jonata Johnson-Hertz, and they have a son, Carlin Jr.

Kathryn K. Howard lives in Rochester, New York. She is a single mother, technical/freelance writer, student, Web editor, and coordinator of *Notes to New York and Washington.*

Ellen Javernick is a first-grade teacher in Loveland, Colorado. She is the author of fifteen children's books and writes for numerous magazines and anthologies. She enjoys playing tennis and spending time with her five children and their families.

Amy Jenkins resides in Wauwatosa, Wisconsin, with her husband, children, and pets. She is a freelance writer and speaker, published in local and national magazines. She has authored two seminars and written a series of articles.

Linda Knight lives in Woodslee, Ontario. She is an inspirational writer. Her published credits include hundreds of greeting card verses, as well as plaques, mugs, shirts, calendars, anthologies, adult and children's devotionals, and magazine articles.

Paul Madison lives in Williamstown, New Jersey. He is an avid sports fan. At forty-six years of age, he realized that the world is too perfect to have been created by a disorganized big bang. Paul is still amazed at God's creation.

Cheryl Norwood lives in Canton, Georgia, just north of Atlanta, with her husband, Mike, in a small World War II bungalow. She has been published in several other anthologies.

Michael T. Powers resides in Janesville, Wisconsin, with his bride, Kristi, and their two boys. He is a motivational speaker, business owner, high school girls' coach, and author.

Julie Saffrin lives in Excelsior, Minnesota. She is a freelance writer of numerous articles and a novelist.

Margaret Saylar attended Westmont College and graduated from California State University at Sacramento. She and her husband, Daniel, have two grown sons. She is the author of more than ten articles.

Karen Strand lives in Lacey, Washington. She is an author, and her articles have appeared in *Moody Magazine*, *Decision*, *Today's Christian Woman*, and *Focus on the Family*.

Janice Thompson of Spring, Texas, is a homeschooling mother of four daughters. She and her husband have a vital interest in teens and youth ministry.

Elizabeth Turner is from Oakville, Ontario, Canada. As a wife, mother, and ICU nurse, Elizabeth uses her writing for personal growth.

D. L. Young resides in the scenic city of Chattanooga, Tennessee, with her husband, daughter, and two precious kitties.

Jeanne Zornes of Wenatchee, Washington, is a conference speaker and widely published author of hundreds of articles and numerous books.

If you enjoyed

Journeys of Friendship,

check out the other books in this series. . .

Journeys of Hope—

30 True Stories of Faith in Adversity
ISBN 1-59310-687-4

Hope is a gift we can offer to each other. Discover how
real individuals turned to God in times of trial and
turned their adversity into hope.

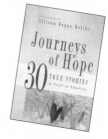

Journeys of Love—

30 True Stories of Undeniable Devotion
ISBN 1-59310-688-2

True expressions of love can change lives forever.
Experience God's desire for us in these thirty true stories
of ordinary individuals whose journeys were changed
by love.

Journeys of Joy—

30 True Stories of Abundant Living
ISBN 1-59310-685-8

Joy is the key to abundant living. If you've simply been
getting by, rediscover the treasure of joy in these true
stories of ordinary men and women.

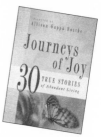